HOOKED ON PHILOSOPHY

HOOKED ON PHILOSOPHY

Thomas Aquinas Made Easy

ROBERT A. O'DONNELL, PhD

ALBA·HOUSE   NEW·YORK

SOCIETY OF ST. PAUL, 2187 VICTORY BLVD., STATEN ISLAND, NEW YORK 10314

Library of Congress Cataloging-in-Publication Data

O'Donnell, Robert A.
    Hooked on Philosophy : St. Thomas Aquinas made easy / Robert A.
    O'Donnell.
        p.   cm.
    Includes bibliographical references and index.
    ISBN 0-8189-0740-1
    1. Thomas Aquinas, Saint, 1225?-1274.   2. Philosophy, Medieval.
    3. Aristotle — Influence.   I. Title.
    B765.T54036   1995
    189'.4 — dc20   95-30850
                                                     CIP

Produced and designed in the United States of America by the
Fathers and Brothers of the Society of St. Paul,
2187 Victory Boulevard, Staten Island, New York 10314,
as part of their communications apostolate.

ISBN: 0-8189-0740-1

© Copyright 1995 by the Society of St. Paul

Printing Information:

Current Printing - first digit	2	3	4	5	6	7	8	9	10

Year of Current Printing - first year shown

			1999		2000

To
John Carr
of the Paulist Fathers
who introduced the author
to
Aristotle and St. Thomas Aquinas
half a century ago

TABLE OF CONTENTS

FOREWORD

The human mind has a natural addiction to know the truth. Attempting to satisfy that addiction is called philosophy. Today, people speak of being "hooked" on drugs, on running, even on phonics. So why not "hooked on philosophy"? It is the most natural of all addictions.

Europeans have been trying to satisfy this addiction for more than 2500 years. Some have succeeded more than others. Some have failed altogether. Still, we call them all philosophers. A philosopher tries to find the truth. He doesn't always succeed. The history of philosophy is a zigzag course which leads away from, and back to the straight line of truth which runs through it. Tracing that straight line of truth, without zigzagging, is very difficult, and few persevere in the effort to do it. Yet, that is what this little book attempts to do.

In Chapter One, the reader will discover how the human imagination and the human mind each contribute to a knowledge of the truth. The imagination is energized by exercise; the mind is fatigued by it. Fairy tales, travel books and novels engage the imagination so that readers frequently find it difficult to put them aside. This book will engage not the reader's imagination, but his mind. It will be necessary to put it aside from time to time to permit the mind to rest itself and to recoup its forces.

Joggers tell us that they break through an exhaustion barrier beyond which they find euphoria. That euphoria hooks them on jogging. Something similar is experienced by philosophers, even amateur philosophers. The gratification which the human mind draws from knowing the truth, i.e. from its insights into the nature of the material universe, into human nature, and into the nature of God, surpasses any euphoria experienced on the level of sensation. Yet, reaching that intellectual barrier and breaking through it can be accomplished only by patient, halting steps. Whoever succeeds in doing it will most certainly be hooked on philosophy.

Technical, philosophical terms have been enclosed within parentheses. They are not necessary to an understanding of the text. They may be of help, however, to the reader who graduates from this book to the works of the philosophers who are cited in the notes.

The author belongs to two families, each of which has been enormously helpful to him in honing the text of this book. To his confreres among the Paulist Fathers, to his sister, Mary Esther Connelly, and to his brothers, William, Edward, and John he expresses his most sincere thanks. He is also most grateful to Father John Sauter of the Archdiocese of Cincinnati, a friend since Louvain days four decades ago, for his invaluable assistance.

New York, 1995

HOOKED ON PHILOSOPHY

1

WHAT WE KNOW AND HOW WE KNOW IT

(EPISTEMOLOGY)

A few facts to begin with (first principles)

The human animal is first linked to its environment by means of sense experiences. And this begins before birth. An expectant mother feels her unborn child stirring in her womb in response to the doctor's prenatal examination or even to the natural movements of her own body. Soon after birth, the baby begins to focus its eyes, as well as its other senses, on a much broadened environment. It becomes interested in everything it senses, beginning with its own body. It cries when hungry or uncomfortable. It smiles when something delights it. After little more than a year of life, it begins to walk and talk. Its first words describe its basic sense experiences: "Mama, Dada, candy, poo-poo. . ." and so forth.

This is the first fact we begin with: All our knowledge originates in *sense experiences.*[1]

For the first half dozen years of its life the child confuses, often quite deliberately, what is real from what is unreal. The imagination works overtime, providing the little child with imaginary friends, pets, places, and so forth. Gradually the child begins to sort out the imaginary from the real. By the time he is ready to begin school, he recognizes the tricks which the imagination can play on him. He is now able to distinguish what is real from what is unreal.

This is our second fact: The real is different from what is non-real.[2]

When the human imagination stops playing tricks on the child, it begins to function in a most useful way. In adulthood, it reproduces for me the sense experiences which I had in the past which I am no longer experiencing. Let us say, for example, that business has required that I travel away from my home for a month. As I prepare to return home, I picture in my imagination not only my wife waiting to welcome me, but the children, the pets, and perhaps even a cozy fire in the living room. All of these are real, individual things which I had experienced with my senses in the past. Ordinarily we say that we have five different external senses: sight, hearing, smell, taste, and touch. It doesn't matter to us here that scientists today tell us that we have many more than five external senses. These remain the five basic areas in which we make sense contact with our environment. The imagination is also a sense, an *internal* sense which processes my external sensations. And there is a second internal sense, the sense memory. For example, as I enter my home following my business trip, I smell a familiar odor which informs me that my wife has prepared my favorite meal, roast beef and hash brown potatoes. I remember the sensation which I had often smelled in the past.

While a human being's knowledge always begins with sense experiences, it does not end there. For of all animals, the human animal alone has a higher power of knowledge which we call the mind or the intellect. It is the function of my human mind to transform the sense images provided to me by my imagination and sense memory. It transforms them from individual images, or images of individual things into ideas which are no longer individual but rather universal.

At this point it is most important that we understand clearly what is meant by a "universal idea." Let us say that in the past I have owned several dogs, among them a German shepherd, a Boston bulldog, and a Mexican Chihuahua. Although they have all died, my imagination continues to supply me with images of them complete to their colors, their shapes, their sizes, even to their barks. These are sense images of individual animals which I can still identify, even by their names: Prince, Pal, and Petunia. Now my mind comes onto the scene and begins to process these sense images. It strips away from the images all the material conditions which make them images of particular, individual dogs, conditions such as their colors, their shapes, their sizes, etc. The mind continues this stripping process until there are no longer individual dogs remaining to which I can assign names. All that is left is the notion "dog," not a German Shepherd or any other breed. My idea "dog" is the idea of a universal dog which exists, never in the real world, but only in my mind. My idea "dog" applies to any dog of any breed which exists now, which has existed in the past, or which will exist in the future anywhere in the real world. My mind forms similar universal ideas of all the individual, material things with which I have had sense contact in the real world.

Here are some examples of my universal ideas: "man," "woman," "potato," "water," "sea level," "golf course." Without the universal ideas which my mind forms, my knowledge would remain on the same level as the knowledge of Prince, Pal, and Petunia. It would be merely sense knowledge. Animals never become scientists. Only people do. And that is because they combine their universal ideas into sentences (propositions) which increase our human knowledge. For example: "Water boils at 212 degrees Fahrenheit at sea level." This sentence (proposition) contains three universal ideas, "water," "degrees" (of heat), and "sea level."

In addition to combining its universal ideas into sentences, the human mind goes a step further and combines these sentences (propositions) into reasoning processes which yield further conclusions. For example: "All water boils at 212 degrees Fahrenheit at sea level. The liquid which I have in this test tube here at the beach is water. Therefore, if I hold this test tube over the fire which I have kindled here on the beach, the water in the test tube will boil when it reaches 212 degrees."

And this brings us to a third fact to begin with: Everything has a sufficient reason, or a cause, for being what it is.[3]

The human mind recognizes spontaneously the connection between an effect and its cause. For example, the fire on the beach is recognized as the cause of the heat which is communicated to the water in the test tube. Another example, I recognize myself as the author, or the cause, of the text printed on this page. Still another, John Wilkes Booth shot Abraham Lincoln at Ford's Theater in Washington, D.C. on April 14, 1865. Booth was the cause of Lincoln's death. One may also say that the gun which he used, and the bullet which entered Lincoln's body, were also causes of the President's death. But the gun did not shoot itself. Booth was the main (principal) cause of Lincoln's death; the gun and bullet were merely instrumental causes of his death.

It is a natural function of the human intellect to link effects which it observes in nature to their causes. The mind begins with the fact (first principle) that everything has a sufficient reason or a cause for being what it is.

Let us now sum up what we have seen so far about what we know and how we know it: We have seen that all human knowledge originates in sense experiences. We have seen further that the human mind is able to distinguish what is real from what is not real. And finally, we have seen that the mind recognizes naturally or spontaneously a whole network of effects linked to their causes in nature.

Two other kinds of ideas

We have described above how the human mind forms universal ideas by stripping away the individuating, material conditions of things. My ideas of "dog," of "house," of "water," and of "sea level" are universal ideas which exist only in my mind. And the human mind forms hundreds of thousands of them in the course of a lifetime. They are most useful to me since they permit me to make such statements as: "Dogs can be trained to protect houses"; "Houses can be constructed of wood or of bricks"; "The Dead Sea in Israel runs to a depth of 1292 feet below sea level which is the lowest point on earth's surface."

Now there are two other kinds of ideas which the human mind forms. The first of these two is a purely quantitative idea which is used in mathematics. Examples of such quantitative ideas are: "one," "two," "three," and so forth, "triangle," "square," "hypotenuse," etc. To form these purely mathematical ideas, the mind must go a step beyond the formation of an ordinary universal idea. It must strip away from the image of any material object, such as a "dog," or a "house," every individuating, material condition with the exception of only one — quantity. Only the notion of quantity now remains in my idea. It is no longer the idea of a dog or a house, or of any other material thing. It is now simply the idea of "one," "ten," "a million," "a square," "a circle," and so forth. Without such ideas as these, none of the mathematical sciences would be possible.

The human mind is capable of taking one final step beyond purely mathematical ideas. It can strip away from the material image even the material condition "quantity." Now what is left? "Being"! It is now an idea merely of "something which exists." It is the idea of "reality," or of the "real." Every healthy human mind forms this idea of being at a very early age, perhaps at two or three. For without this idea of the "real," the child could not distinguish what is real from what is unreal. Of course, the child is unaware that its young mind has formed the idea of being. And most people go through life, even a very long life, without ever becoming aware that their minds have formed this fascinating idea of being. Another way to say this is that most people never, from the cradle to the grave, reflect on how their minds work. Still another way to say it is that very, very few people, in their lifetimes, become philosophers. This book can change that for you.

Who is "The Philosopher"?

To qualify as a "philosopher," a person does not have to give a true or authentic explanation of the real world. One need only try to do so. Through twenty-five centuries of Western thought, many have tried and are therefore called "philosophers." But only a few have succeeded. What shall we call these few? Sages, perhaps?

The Sage of sages was a Greek named Aristotle who died about 325 years before Christ was born. Aristotle's greatest disciple was St. Thomas Aquinas, a Dominican friar, who lived for forty-nine years in the thirteenth century. Sixteen centuries separated Thomas from Aristotle. Thomas called Aristotle simply "The Philosopher"; no one else, he deemed, was worthy of that title.

Because of these two great thinkers, the philosophy which is being placed before you in this book has come to be known as "Aristotelian-Thomistic" philosophy. It is also called "realism" because it makes a clear, crisp distinction between the human person, who is the knower, and the real world which he knows. It holds that even if Aristotle and St. Thomas, and you, the reader of this book, had never been born, still the real world would have existed.

There are many so-called philosophers who do not accept this way of thinking. We have said that all human knowledge begins with sense experiences, but that it does not end with sense experiences. That is the teaching of Aristotle and of St. Thomas Aquinas. David Hume, the English philosopher (1711-1776) maintains that human knowledge begins and ends on the level of sense experience.

We have also said that the human mind is distinct from the real world which it knows. Another way of saying this is that the human mind does not create: it merely discovers the real world which it knows. That, too, is the teaching of Aristotle and St. Thomas Aquinas. But Immanuel Kant, the German philosopher (1724-1804), teaches that the so-called real world is an amorphous, unstructured reality, upon which the human mind, in knowing it, imposes form and structure. Kant would say that such "forms" or "categories" as "cause and effect," as "substance," and as "quality" are imposed by the human mind on unstructured reality, much the same as a baker uses cookie cutters to shape the dough before baking his biscuits.

Hume and Kant were accomplished philosophers, but they were not sages. Aristotle was a sage. He is "The Philosopher"!

2

A REFLECTION ON OUR IDEA OF BEING
(METAPHYSICS)

Being as Being

In Chapter One we said that every human intellect forms the notion or idea of being at a very young age. This idea enables the person to distinguish what is real from what is not real, being from non-being. We said, too, that the mind forms countless universal ideas of particular kinds of beings, e.g. human beings, animal beings, inanimate beings, and so forth. But our idea of being lies beyond all our universal ideas; it is not an idea of any particular kind of being. It is not the idea of human being, not the idea of animal being, not the idea of inanimate being, it is simply the idea of "being as being." It is the idea of "being period!" It is the idea of "existence," the idea of "the real." It is the idea which prompts us to ask the question: "What does it mean 'to be'?" "What does it mean 'to exist'?" "What does it mean 'to be something real'?" These are three different ways of asking the same question. And that is the question which we shall try to answer in this chapter. What can we say about our idea of "being as being"?

What we are doing now is something that only philosophers (metaphysicians) do. We are reflecting upon the idea of being which our minds have formed. As we have said, all minds form this idea, and everyone uses it to distinguish what is real from what is not real, but almost no one reflects upon this idea and talks about it, as we are about to do.

The First Philosophers (Metaphysicians)

The very first person who reflected upon and talked about the idea of being was a Greek by the name of Parmenides who was born 515 years before Christ. His reflection went like this: I have two ways of knowing things, with my senses and with my mind. Obviously, my mind is the higher of these two powers. I must therefore accept the evidence which my mind presents to me. And if my senses present evidence which contradicts the evidence which my mind presents, then I must reject the evidence presented by my senses. And this is in fact the case. With my senses I observe that everything in the world is moving both in space and in time; everything is in a process of becoming other than it is. On the other hand, my mind tells me that everything which is, is being; nothing is becoming other than it is. "Being" is the material of which the whole universe is made; it is spatially extended, and therefore there is no such thing as empty space. And if there is no empty space, there is no movement possible.

Parmenides had a student whose name was Zeno. He was 25 years younger than his teacher, and a bit more inventive. To prove Parmenides was right, and that the whole idea of change or motion is ridiculous, Zeno described a race between a young Greek athlete named Achilles and a turtle. The turtle is given a head start, and poor Achilles never manages to catch up with him. Why? Well, Zeno explains, Achilles must first reach the starting line from which the turtle departed. When he gets there, the turtle has advanced farther. And when Achilles gets to that farther point, the turtle has advanced still farther. Achilles continues to reduce the distance between himself and his opponent, but he never succeeds in catching or passing him. Zeno's purpose in presenting this and other similar arguments is to show that space and time contain contradictions, and therefore they cannot be as our senses perceive them to be.

Now we recognize right away that something is very wrong with Parmenides' and Zeno's view of the universe. But what? Another Greek, a contemporary of Parmenides, thought that he had the answer. Heraclitus (535-475 B.C.) agreed with Parmenides that we have two human powers with which to know things: the senses and the intellect. He agreed further that the senses report to us that everything in the universe is in a constant state of flux. Everything is becoming. True, too, is Parmenides' observation that the human mind tells us that none of this is accurate. According to the mind, everything is being, nothing is becoming. "Aha," says Heraclitus, "the human mind is the culprit; it deceived Parmenides and it's always trying to deceive the rest of us. There is no such thing as being. Everything is continually becoming." "You cannot walk down into the same river twice," Heraclitus told his students. One of these students, Cratylus by name, added emphasis to his Master's teaching by proclaiming: "You cannot walk down into the same river once!"

Now just a minute! That can't be true either. How are we going to find a solution to this problem of "being and becoming"? A hundred and fifty years after Parmenides and Heraclitus left the scene, still another great Greek, Aristotle (384-322 B.C.) appeared and discovered the solution. Parmenides and Heraclitus were each partly right and partly wrong. We must accept the evidence both of our senses and of our intellect. The evidences they present to us do not contain any contradictions. The senses link us to our environment while the intellect gives us a more profound understanding of it. What the earlier Greeks did not recognize was that there is a middle ground between being and becoming. Aristotle calls it "being in potency." Every being which we experience with our senses contains potency to become other than it now is.

Potency is the capacity to change which all objects of our sense experience contain. For example, back in the year 1498 when Michelangelo was 23 years of age, he selected a large, flawless block of Carrara marble from the mountains of Northern Italy. By 1501 he had carved it into the exquisite statue of the Virgin Mary holding the crucified body of her son in her arms, the Pietà, which has been on display for almost 500 years at St. Peter's Basilica in Rome. Before Michelangelo took his chisel in hand, the "being-in-act" which he had in his studio was a block of Carrara marble. But that same block of marble was, in potency, the beautiful Pietà. The same block of marble contained the potencies to become countless other statues, had only Michelangelo chosen to carve them rather than the Pietà. He might have carved, for example, Marcus Aurelius astride his horse, or a bust of Julius Caesar or ten million other subjects. The block of Carrara marble contained all these potencies within itself before the Artist "actualized" that one single potency which fashioned it into the Virgin Mary tenderly cradling the dead body of her son in her arms.

Sixteen hundred years after Aristotle first proposed his philosophical theory of "potency and act," St. Thomas Aquinas broadened it to include every conceivable type of change which can take place in the material universe. That which is "in act" — e.g., a chicken's egg, is, at the same time, "in potency" a live chick. The acorn "in act" is at the same time a towering oak "in potency." If I am a recognized nuclear physicist "in act," I may be many things "in potency" which I have not yet become, including perhaps a fiddle player. St. Thomas Aquinas says it this way: "Nothing can be changed, modified, or affected in any way unless it has within itself some principle (potency) which can receive the new modification."[4]

 St. Thomas also says that, taken together, our ideas of potency

and act are co-extensive with our idea of being as being. Another *NB*
way to say this is: Our ideas of potency and act, taken together,
encompass all existing beings, for whatever exists is either pure act,
unmixed with potency, or it is a mixture of potency and act.

Both Aristotle and St. Thomas explain that potency is that
part of a being which receives the act, and, in receiving it, limits it.
The act, on the other hand, is that part of a being which makes it *quality*
the kind of a being it is. The potency of a stone cannot receive the *of being*
act of a human being. In other words, there must be a proportion
between any act and the potency which receives it. If there exists
a "pure act," i.e. an act which is not received by any potency, that
particular act will be completely unlimited (infinite). Another
name for pure act is God. (See Chapter Three)

Now let us see how this Aristotelian-Thomistic theory of
potency and act helps us to understand better our idea of being as
being. To begin with, it shows us that our idea of being is not, as
Parmenides thought, the idea of something static, the inert material of which the whole universe is made which eliminates the
possibility of any change whatsoever. Rather, Aristotle and St.
Thomas have shown us that our idea of being is the idea of a
dynamic reality which, though it has the stable core of being, is
continually becoming. They have shown us that being and becoming can co-exist in a cosmic harmony. These two great philosophers
have also shown us that our idea of being is not, as Heraclitus
thought, a meaningless, misleading idea. It is a most authentic idea
which we draw from our sense experiences in the material world,
and which makes it possible for us, by reapplying it, to probe to the
marvelous mysteries of the real world of which we are a part.

Essence and Existence[5]

Every real thing has an essence. The essence is what makes the
thing to be the particular type of thing which it is. In the Latin

language, another word for essence is "quidditas" which, in English, is translated "whatness." A stone has the essence or the whatness of a stone. It is different from the essence of a rose or the essence of a human being. The essence of anything is its potency which must receive an act in order to exist in the real world. But the essence (potency) of a stone cannot receive the act of a rose, nor can the essence (potency) of a human being receive the act of a stone. There is always a proper proportion between the essence of anything and the act of existence which brings it into the real order.

Now our ideas exist only in our minds, for example our idea of being as being, our ideas of potency and act, our ideas of essence and existence. They do not exist in the real world as such. Everything which exists in the real world is a particular, individual thing. But our ideas are not particular or individual; they are universal. Still, our ideas are most useful to us since they give us a deeper understanding of the particular, individual things in the real world. But in order to serve this useful purpose, our ideas must be reapplied (predicated) to the real world from which we got them in the first place. Remember that all our human knowledge originates in sense experiences of the real world.

Let us take, for example, the idea of being as being, which is the most universal idea the human mind is capable of forming. It is our most universal idea because we can reapply it to absolutely everything which exists: to God, to angels, to humans, to animals, to inanimate things, and to any individual within any of these classifications of beings. But every time we reapply (predicate) our idea of being to something in the real world, we do it in a way that is partly the same and partly different in each case. In other words, our idea of being is never reapplied to any two real beings in the real world in a way that is completely the same. Even in the case of identical twins or of two peas in a pod, each individual has an essence all its own which makes it a different being from its twin.

True, they are partly the same. A pebble on the beach and the Pope are partly the same in that they are both real beings. They both exist. But they are obviously very different from one another. And when we predicate our idea of being of them, we must predicate it in a way that is partly the same and partly different. Philosophers call this "the analogical predication of the concept of being as being."[6]

The Causes of Being

We shall continue here to reflect upon and talk about our idea of being as being. We have already seen that it is not an idea of something static. On the contrary, it is the idea of a dynamic reality which is shared by everyone and everything which exists beginning with God who is pure act and totally unlimited (see Chapter Three) and extending to all other beings each of which is composed of an act and a potency. Of the zillions of such beings which exist, we have said that no two of them are identical. Each has its own individual essence or "whatness" which makes it different from every other individual being. That is why, when I begin reapplying (predicating) my idea of being to things in the real world, I must do so in a way that is partly the same and partly different in each case.

We also said in Chapter One that it is a natural function of the human mind to recognize the connection between the individual beings which it knows and the causes of those beings. John Wilkes Booth, his gun, and the bullet which he shot from that gun into President Lincoln's body can all three be described as the causes of Lincoln's death. Booth was the main or principal "efficient" cause, while his gun and the bullet were each a contributing or instrumental "efficient" cause of the President's death. An "efficient" cause is an agent which, by its action, produces in some way or other the effect. The assassin, the assassin's gun, and the bullet were all agents which, by their action, brought about the effect; all three can therefore be called "efficient" causes.

Now there are other kinds of causes. The motivation which John Wilkes Booth had for killing Lincoln is called the final cause of the President's death. The "final cause" is the reason why an agent (an efficient cause) acts to produce an effect. Although it may sound like a contradiction in terms, we can say that the "final" cause is the "first" of all causes, because without the final cause there would no causality whatsoever. St. Thomas says this in an almost poetic fashion: "The end (the final cause) is the cause of causes because it is the cause of the causality in all causes."[7] So the final cause is the motivation, the purpose, the goal, the end, which the efficient cause has in mind before it begins to act, before it exercises its causality. That is why we can call it the "first" cause. But we can also call it the "last" cause, since it is the goal which is accomplished only after the efficient cause produces the effect.

The Order of Intention

In Chapter One we said that my universal ideas, my ideas of "dog" and "car" for example, exist only in my mind, never in the real world. Real beings are always individual real beings; they are never universal beings. Nevertheless, my mind is a part of me, and I am an individual being who exists in the real world. So it is not precisely correct to say that universal ideas do not exist in the real world. They are contained in my mind and are therefore a part of the real world. Still, they are a unique part of the real world, unlike any other part of it. To explain how our ideas are part of the real world, Aristotle and St. Thomas make a distinction between "the order of intention" and "the order of execution." The order of intention is that part of the real world in which mental activity takes place, in other words the intellect. The order of execution is that part of the real world where physical activity takes place. St. Thomas then says that the final cause is first in the order of intention while it is last in the order of execution.[8]

Let us see this in an example. In 1932, the New York Yankees were at Wrigley Field in Chicago to play the Cubs in the third game of baseball's World Series. With the score tied, Babe Ruth was the batter. Before the Cub's pitcher could throw the ball, Ruth stepped away from the plate and turned to face the fans in the grandstand. Slowly, he lifted his left arm and pointed to a spot on the outfield fence 400 feet away. He then stepped up to the plate and blasted the next pitch over the fence at that precise point.

Though there is some controversy about this today, let us say for the sake of argument that before he swung the bat, "home run" was in Babe Ruth's order of intention. After he had driven the ball over the fence, the "Bambino" was credited with a home run in the order of execution. Babe Ruth was clearly the efficient cause of that unforgettable home run. The final cause of it was his desire to win that game by hitting a home run. Without that final cause, he would not have become the efficient cause of the home run. (The Babe's bat was, of course, the instrumental efficient cause of the famous hit.)

Taken together, the efficient cause and the final cause are classified as "extrinsic causes." Extrinsic means "outside of." What are these two causes outside of? They are outside of the effect. Sailing over Wrigley Field's outfield fence, the ball which Ruth hit was the effect of that act of causality. Babe Ruth, his bat, and his motivation for hitting that home run are all different from and "extrinsic to" the ball sailing over the fence.

The reason we are now talking about extrinsic causes is that there are also "intrinsic causes." If extrinsic causes are outside the effect, intrinsic causes are, of course, inside the effect.

Now when we talk about effects, we are talking about all real beings which exist with the exception of God (pure act). We have said that all beings which are not pure act (God) are composites of potency and act. And St. Thomas explains that "nothing is changed from potency to act except by an agent which is itself already in act."[9] That is another way of saying that every being which is composed of potency and act (and that includes every being except God) is an effect of causes. So we see that, just as potency and act, taken together, are coextensive with the idea of being, so also are cause and effect, taken together, coextensive with the idea of being. And any mathematician will tell us that two things which are coextensive with the same thing are also coextensive with each other. This means that whether we are speaking of "potency and act," or of "cause and effect," or of "being as being" we are speaking about precisely the same thing: all of the real world, every real being in it.

Now let us return to intrinsic causes. We have seen that all real beings which exist outside the human mind are individual real beings. All of our human knowledge begins with our sense experiences of these real individual beings. And they are all made out of matter. Our external senses can make contact only with material beings. All the material beings with which I have sense experiences have this in common: they are all made out of matter. Yet I have sense experiences with a great variety of material things. Some of them are alive, like insects, animals, and people. Many of them are not alive, like grains of sand, rocks, raindrops, and musical instruments. They are all made out of matter, but they are all very different from one another. So besides the matter which makes them like one another, they must contain another ingredient, something which makes them different from one another. Aristotle and St. Thomas call this second ingredient of material beings "form." These are the two internal causes of material (corporeal) being: *matter and form*. It is the matter which causes them all to be similar to one another; it is the form which causes them all to be different from one another. Further, matter is potency, form is act. It is the matter which, as potency, receives the form which is the act. The matter limits the form, the form causes the matter to be a particular kind of material being. We see here a point of intersection between the theory of potency and act on the one hand, and the internal causes of material being on the other. Mice, and men, and minerals are all material beings and in that they are like one another. But they are very different from one another because they have very different kinds of forms. Mice have non-intelligent animal forms, men have intelligent animal forms, and minerals have forms which are non-vegetative, non-animal, and non-intelligent.

So now we have four causes, two of them extrinsic (the efficient and the final causes), and two of them intrinsic (the material and the formal causes). Among philosophers centuries of use have consecrated the phrase "The Four Causes." And yet there are more than four. We have talked above of two kinds of efficient causes: the principal efficient cause (Babe Ruth) and the instrumental efficient cause (his bat). Aristotle and St. Thomas mention a second kind of formal cause. They call it the "exemplary cause." The easiest way of knowing what an exemplary cause is, is by means of an example. An architect who designs a house must draw a plan of the house which he turns over to the contractor. Even before he draws the plan, the architect must have in his imagination a model or an "exemplar" of what he wishes the contractor to build. This image of the house is the exemplary cause of the plan which the architect produces. That plan, in its turn, becomes the exemplary cause of the house which the contractor builds.

We are gradually unfolding the content of our idea of being. Next we must consider the classifications of being which Aristotle and St. Thomas call:

The Categories of Being[10]

Because our idea of being is the most universal idea which the human mind is capable of forming, philosophers give it a special name. They call it a "transcendental" idea. This means that it stands above all our other universal ideas, and can be reapplied (predicated) to absolutely every real being without exception. And it is no exaggeration to say that there are countless numbers of these real beings in existence. There are approximately 5 billion human beings presently living on this planet, and there are many times that number of insects, birds, and animals inhabiting the earth. Besides these, every grain of sand on every beach anywhere in the world is an individual real being with its own essence. All these beings, and countless other ones which we have not mentioned here, are somehow contained in my transcendental idea of being as being. And our minds classify them all into just two categories: "substances" and "accidents." A *substance* is defined as a real being which exists by itself, independent of all other beings. Substances can be living or non-living. A flea is a substance. An apple tree is a substance. A rock is a substance. We can also call such things as automobiles and airplanes substances, though they are really many different substances which have been brought together to form a vehicle. *Accidents*, on the other hand, are real beings which cannot exist by themselves. They can exist only in a substance. An example will make this distinction between substances and accidents clear: the color of my skin is real being, but it cannot exist apart from me, apart from my substance. Similarly, my weight, my shape, the fact that I am my father's son, all of my thoughts, my age, my nationality, all of these things are part of the real world because they are part of me, but no one of them can exist by itself apart from my human substance.

Aristotle was the first to list nine different kinds of accidents: quantity, quality, relation, action, passion, place, time, posture, and habit. Let us try to give a single example which embraces all nine of these accidents simultaneously, and substance as well, bringing the grand total of categories illustrated in our example to ten: Abraham Lincoln was a tall white lawyer who often wore a top hat and who, as President of the United States, freed the slaves, and was, while sitting in a box at Ford's Theater, murdered by John Wilkes Booth in 1865.

Substance:	Abraham Lincoln
Quantity:	tall
Quality:	white
Relation:	to his murderer
Action:	freed the slaves
Passion:	was murdered
Time:	1865
Place:	Ford's Theater
Posture:	sitting
Habit:	top hat

We should note that relation is unlike the other eight accidents in that it orders the substance in which it inheres to something outside itself. Every substance has many relations ordering it to things outside itself. For example, I am a substance who is related to my parents, to my employer, to my Church, to my house, to the personal computer which I am presently using as a word processor, and on and on and on. Jonathan Swift in his *On Poetry*, wrote: "So naturalists observe, a flea hath smaller fleas that on him prey; and these have smaller still to bite 'em. And so proceed *ad infinitum*." The real world is an intricate web of relations which link together countless individual beings. Of these myriads, there is no single being which is totally unrelated to any other individual being. Moreover, act and potency are related mutually to one another. Causes are related to the effects which they produce.

About the two accidents, action and passion, action is whatever the substance does. My singing is classified as an action. Passion is whatever is done to the substance. My appendectomy is classified as a passion. By habit, Aristotle means whatever is attached to a substance, such as the clothing which humans wear.

We see now how these categories or classifications of real beings add still another dimension to our idea of being as being. And this added dimension helps us to probe a little more deeply into the mystery which is the real world.

Other Names for Being (The Transcendentals)

Reflecting upon our idea of being as being has led us to recognize parts of the real world which otherwise might have escaped our attention: potency and act, for example; essence and existence; the causes of being; the categories of being. All of these are contained in our idea of being. Now we ask: Are there any other terms which, like the name "being," also include all these parts of the real world, all these realities? Aristotle and St. Thomas speak of three such terms: unity, truth, and goodness. Let us consider each one of these three in turn.

Unity[11]

We have said that only individual beings exist in the real world. A universal dog exists only in my mind as an idea, never in the real world. If we wish to be precise, we must say that even universal ideas are parts of the real world since they do exist in my mind which is, itself, a part of the real world. But even a universal idea is one, individual idea, and it must be so in order to exist at all. So we say that there is a oneness or a unity in every real being. And our idea of "unity" is exactly the same as our idea of "being." Why then speak of it? Because it helps us to understand a little more fully our idea of being. Unity brings out clearly the fact that being is undivided. St. Thomas explains it this way. Every real being, he says, is either uncomposed (simple) or composed of parts. If it has no parts, if it is uncomposed, then it is, of course, one. It has unity. If it has parts, as all material beings do, those parts must be united in order for that being to exist. When a composed being falls apart, that is to say when its parts separate from one another, that being ceases to exist.

Parmenides, you will recall, was so impressed with the unity of being, that he declared that everything real is one and the same (monism), and that such a thing as movement in space and time — in fact change of any kind whatsoever — is merely an illusion. Parmenides got himself into this trouble by confusing mathematical unity with the unity of being (transcendental unity). The difference between these two kinds of unity is simply this: mathematical unity applies only to material beings which are quantitative. The unity we are talking about here applies to all beings, whether material or not. That is why it is called, just as being is called, "transcendental."

Truth

Truth is another name for being when we speak of being as it is known by an intellect. As we have seen, the human mind forms ideas of real beings which we first experience on the level of sensation. These ideas are said to be "true" when they correspond accurately to the real beings as they exist outside my mind. In Chapter Three we shall speak about the mind of God. If we accept that God does exist, that He is intelligent, and further that He is the cause or the creator of the real world and everything in it, then we see clearly that being must somehow be related not only to human minds, but also to the divine mind. As humans, we know real beings which we have not caused or created. God, however, knows everything which He has created. Just as an architect must have an image or, as we said earlier, an exemplary cause, of the building he designs, so too God must have some kind of foreknowledge of what He creates. Creation, or the real world, is said to be "true" because it corresponds to the exemplary ideas in God's mind in imitation of which He created it. So recognizing truth as another name for being gives us a still fuller knowledge of what is contained in our idea of being.

Goodness

Just as truth is another name for being when we speak of being as related to an intellect, goodness is another name for being when we speak of being as related to a free will. Aristotle and St. Thomas say that "the good is what everyone desires." Goodness expresses being insofar as it is desirable. We have already seen that final causality, i.e., the reason why an efficient cause produces an effect, is a part of our idea of being. If goodness is another name for being, then we can say that being is what everyone desires, and as such it is the final cause of all causality. Remember that poetic line from the writings of St. Thomas: "The end (the final cause) is the cause of causes because it is the cause of the causality in all causes." We can now paraphrase St. Thomas by saying: "Goodness or being is the cause of causes because it is the cause of the causality in all causes." It is what everyone desires.

A Word about Beauty

Some philosophers hold that "beauty" is also another name for being. St. Thomas defines beauty in three Latin words: "Quae visa placent."[12] This is translated: "Those things which, when seen, please." St. Thomas might have said: ". . . when seen, heard, smelled, tasted, or touched." In other words, beauty is what delights our senses. And therefore the objects which we find beautiful must always be material objects. If we accept this restricted meaning of beauty, it is clear that beauty cannot be another name for being, since being also includes immaterial objects such as God and angels. We have said that goodness appeals to the human will, and that everyone desires to possess what is good. By contrast, beauty appeals to the human intellect. Beauty is even defined by some philosophers as "the good of the intellect." If we accept this less restricted meaning of beauty, perhaps we can include it among the other names for being. In any case, beauty seems to be related to both truth and goodness, and it is most certainly included in the idea of being.

A Word about Evil[13]

St. Thomas Aquinas says: "One opposite is known through the other, as darkness is known through light; similarly, what evil is must be known from the nature of 'the good'."[14] Since we have just discussed goodness, this seems the appropriate place to add a word about evil.

There are two kinds of evil: physical evil and moral evil. Here, we are interested only in physical evil. Moral evil, which refers to human behavior, will be treated in Chapter Six. Examples of physical evil are blindness, cancer, and the like. Physical evil can be defined as the absence of a good where that good should be; the absence of sight, for example, in any human being. Accordingly, we cannot say that evil is "being"; rather it is the absence of being where being should be. Nor can we say that physical evil is "nothing," since it is clearly recognizable as existing in the material universe. But what is physical evil from one point of view may be seen as a physical good from another point of view. From the rabbit's point of view, it is certainly an evil to be eaten by a fox. But the fox views it differently.

We have quoted Aristotle and St. Thomas as saying that "the good is what everyone desires." No agent, whether animal or human, chooses evil. Only the good can motivate an agent; only the good can act as a final cause. But sometimes an agent may think something to be good which is really evil. In this case, the agent becomes the efficient cause of the evil indirectly (*per accidens*).

Can God be the cause of the physical evil which we experience in the universe? Only indirectly (*per accidens*). In creating the cycle of living beings which is a good, God wills indirectly that the rabbit be eaten by the fox. On a broader scale, we may say that God, in causing a higher good, for example the good of the whole material universe, causes indirectly (*per accidens*) the corruption of all material beings. And from the point of view of the individual, material being, this corruption is seen as a physical evil. To recall St. Thomas' words: "What evil is must be known from the nature of the good."

3

DOES GOD EXIST AND
WHAT CAN WE KNOW ABOUT HIM?

(THEODICY)

Ideas about God

Everybody has something to say about God. A few people say that He does not exist (atheism). Some in the past have said that there are many gods (polytheism). Jews, Christians, and Moslems say that there is only one God (monotheism). Today, the New Age people identify God with themselves and with the world in which they live (pantheism). Still others says that if God exists, human beings can know nothing whatsoever about Him (agnosticism). The fact that everybody has something to say about God is itself an argument for His existence. This argument is stated briefly as follows: "The entire human race has always and everywhere believed that a superior being (or beings) exists upon whom the material world and everything in it depend." The fact that there are a few atheists who deny the validity of this argument, merely brings the argument into sharper focus. For it is, after all, the exception which proves the rule. Traditionally, this first argument for God's existence has been called "the argument from the universal consent of mankind."

The very first fact which we began with in Chapter One is that all our human knowledge originates in our sense experiences. We also said that the human mind recognizes spontaneously the connection between an effect and its cause. If we accept these first facts (first principles), then we must expect that any argument which we formulate for the existence of God will begin with our sense experiences, and will see God as the cause of them and of us.

But not everyone accepts these first principles. Some philosophers have held that we are born with certain ideas (innate ideas). Aristotle and St. Thomas deny this. They maintain that the human mind is a blank slate (*tabula rasa*) upon which nothing at all is written until we begin to have sense experiences. Some philosophers hold that one of the ideas we are born with is the idea of God. And upon this innate idea of God they build a very appealing argument for His existence. No one has expressed this argument more clearly than St. Anselm (1033-1109) who was the Archbishop of Canterbury (England). Called "the ontological argument," St. Anselm thought of it as the argument to end all arguments. It can be stated as follows:

> God is the greatest being thinkable.
> The greatest being thinkable cannot exist only in my mind.
> He must also exist outside my mind.
> If He existed only in my mind, He would not be the greatest being thinkable, for I can think of a being who exists both inside my mind and outside my mind.
> Therefore God must exist outside my mind as well as inside my mind.

A contemporary of St. Anselm, a Catholic monk named Gaunilo, challenged the argument suggesting that since we can have an idea of the most beautiful island thinkable, that such an island must exist somewhere in the world. But Gaunilo was no match for the

Archbishop of Canterbury. Anselm answered Gaunilo that his idea of God was the idea of a totally unlimited (infinite) being while the idea of an island is the idea of a limited (finite) being. A totally unlimited (infinite) being must possess the perfection of existence; otherwise, it would be limited. On the other hand, any limited being, such as the most beautiful island thinkable, may or may not exist.

A hundred and sixty years later, St. Thomas Aquinas took the side of Gaunilo. St. Anselm's ontological argument cannot be accepted, he said, because it makes an unjustified leap from what is inside the mind to what is outside the mind.[15] But since St. Thomas' time, several well known philosophers have taken the side of St. Anselm. For example, the French philosopher, René Descartes (1596-1650), taught that any idea which we have which is "clear and distinct" corresponds to a real object existing outside the mind. We do have, he maintained, such a "clear and distinct" idea of an absolutely perfect being. Therefore God, who is an absolutely perfect being, does exist.

Gottfried Wilhelm Leibniz (1646-1716), the German philosopher, was four years old when Descartes died. Leibniz put the argument in a slightly different way: It is at least possible that God exists since our idea of Him as the infinite being contains no contradictions. And if God is possible, He must exist since existence is a part of our idea of Him.

Another famous German philosopher, Immanuel Kant (1724-1804), who was born eight years after Leibniz died, gave Anselm's argument still another twist: the human intellect cannot know that God exists by manipulating ideas. But we know with certitude that God exists because of the compelling force with which the moral law imposes itself upon our consciousness. What others call "conscience," Kant called "the categorical imperative." We know that the moral law must be obeyed, and the moral law makes no sense at all unless God exists.

Closer to our own time, Cardinal John Henry Newman (1801-1890), found the argument from conscience for God's existence the most persuasive. The most distinguished English intellectual of the 19th century, Newman was one of the Anglican clergymen involved in the "Oxford Movement" which attempted to revitalize the Anglican Church by reviving certain Roman Catholic doctrines and rituals. Newman was received into the Catholic Church in 1845. He was ordained to the Catholic priesthood the following year, and created a Cardinal by Pope Leo XIII in 1879. His cause for sainthood is presently being examined by the Vatican. Newman's profound sense of moral responsibility led him to acknowledge the existence of God as the supreme lawgiver without whom there can be no moral law. Newman's "conscience" and Kant's "categorical imperative" are two sides of the same coin: conscience focuses on human freedom responding to divine law. The categorical imperative focuses on the divine law commanding human freedom. Such proofs as these relate as much to the human will as to the human intellect.

The Five Ways

Let us return now to the thought of St. Thomas Aquinas. Remember that he starts with the fact that all our knowledge originates in sense experiences, and with the further fact that it is a natural function of the human mind to link effects which it encounters in nature to their causes. Based upon these two principles, St. Thomas offers us Five Ways of proving that God exists. All five of these proofs occupy only a single page of his principal work, the *Summa Theologica*.[16] Yet rivers of ink have been used by those who have written commentaries on *The Five Ways*. We shall try to imitate St. Thomas by stating them briefly here.

Each of the Five Ways takes as its point of departure a sense experience which everybody has in the material world. The *First Way* begins with the sense experience of motion or change in the universe. As we said in Chapter Two, St. Thomas considers motion or change as any passage from potency to act. This first of his five proofs St. Thomas borrowed from Aristotle[17] and can be stated as follows: We observe that things in the world move. Now whatever moves, is moved by another, for nothing can move itself. Another way to say this is that whatever moves from potency to act must be so moved by an agent which is already itself in act. And if that agent is in its turn also moved, it must be moved by still another agent which is itself already in act. An infinite series of such movers is impossible. We must eventually arrive at a first mover which is itself unmoved. And everyone understands this to be God. An example may clarify this First Way. In a long, moving train, each car is moved by the car immediately in front of it. Yet at the very front there must be an engine which pulls along all the cars behind it. Without the engine which we can call the first car, there could be no second or third or fourth car. Obviously, this example limps since the engine is not a first, unmoved mover. The fact that the engine is also, like the cars behind it, a moved mover, simply means that we have not yet reached the beginning of that series of movers. We have not yet arrived at the first, unmoved mover.

But does this First Way really prove the existence of God? It proves the existence of a first unmoved mover. It does not prove the existence of a personal, intelligent unmoved mover. Nor does the Second Way, which is very similar to the First Way. Instead of beginning with motion, the *Second Way* begins with efficient causes producing effects. For example, Babe Ruth was the efficient cause of that 1932 home run at Wrigley Field. This argument also invokes the impossibility of an infinite series of causes and effects, and concludes to the existence of a first uncaused cause. But is this

God? St. Thomas says that everybody says so. But is this first
uncaused cause the personal, intelligent, free Creator in whom
most of us believe? Perhaps not, but there are still three more Ways.

A Word About Ways One and Two

St. Thomas' first two Ways of demonstrating the existence of
God are not really different from one another. For, as we have
already seen in Chapter Two, every time an efficient cause produces
an effect, there is movement from potency to act. And on the other
hand, every time a mover moves something, that mover is exercis-
ing causality. Taken together, these two Ways reason to the
existence of a first cause which is itself uncaused. This first uncaused
cause is called the "primary" cause. All other efficient causes are
called "secondary" causes. And secondary causes are always effects
of other causes. What the first two Ways show clearly is that we
cannot have a series of secondary causes which never arrives at a
primary cause. Without the primary cause, which is itself uncaused,
there can be no secondary causes.

The Third Way

To understand St. Thomas' Third Way, we must first understand the meaning of two terms: (1) contingent being, and (2)
necessary being. A contingent being is a being which begins to exist
at some point in time or which ceases to exist at some subsequent
point in time. A necessary being, on the other hand, is a being
which always exists, a being which never begins to be nor ever
passes out of existence. Another way to present this distinction
between a contingent and a necessary being is to say that a
contingent being may exist or it may not exist, while a necessary

being must exist, cannot not exist. A contingent being does not exist necessarily.

The *Third Way* can be stated as follows: We observe continually in nature beings coming into existence and passing out of existence, i.e., contingent beings. Therefore, a necessary being must exist who brings these contingent beings into existence. If there were a time when no such necessary being existed — a time, in other words, when nothing at all existed — then nothing would exist now. For nothing can bring itself into existence; to do this it would have to have existed before it existed. This is simply another way of saying that nothing can be moved from potency to act except by an agent which is itself already in act.

This Third Way is really the fundamental proof for God's existence. For when we speak of "beings which are moved" or of "beings which are caused," we are speaking, of course, of contingent beings. In the Fourth and Fifth Ways, St. Thomas speaks of "degrees of perfection" and of "natural bodies which lack intelligence." Obviously, these, too, are contingent beings.

The Fourth and Fifth Ways

The *Fourth Way* begins with the degrees of perfection which we observe in the world. We express these degrees of perfection by comparing one thing to another. For example, someone might say that Princess Grace of Monaco was a more beautiful woman than Eleanor Roosevelt. Or, the sun is 332,000 times larger than the earth. These degrees of perfection which are found in contingent beings, St. Thomas reasons, necessarily imply the existence of a maximum perfection which is found in a necessary, supreme being. And this supreme being which possesses all perfections without any limitations must be seen as the cause of all the perfections found in other beings.

As we saw at the end of Chapter Two, "truth" and "goodness" are other names for "being." And since we observe in the world degrees of truth and goodness in contingent beings, there must be a supreme being who is the cause of being and goodness and truth in all other beings. And this supreme being, St. Thomas concludes, we call God.

This Fourth Way brings us a step beyond the first three Ways. For one of the created perfections which we observe in the world is intelligence. And another is the human person. Now the supreme being cannot cause these perfections in other beings unless He first possesses them in His own being, and possesses them in a totally unlimited (infinite) manner. So we have now reached a personal, intelligent, first, necessary, uncaused cause. And this being everyone certainly calls God.

The *Fifth Way* begins with the observation that we frequently see in the world beings which lack intelligence acting for a specific end or purpose. It is clear that this does not happen by chance but by design. Now beings which lack intelligence obviously cannot move toward an end unless they are directed to that end by a being who possesses intelligence. St. Thomas gives the example of an arrow which is shot toward a target by an archer. And he concludes that "therefore some intelligent being exists by which all natural things are directed to their ends; and this being we call God."

This Fifth Way, like the Fourth, also proves the existence of an *intelligent* supreme being. St. Thomas' example of the archer directing his arrow to the target seems a rather feeble example when compared to the phenomenon of instinct within the animal kingdom. A bird of a particular species will always instinctively build its nest of the same materials in the same way so as to insure its own and its offsprings' welfare. Some animals hibernate while others migrate to survive the severity of winter seasons. These instinctive behavior patterns must be attributed to an intelligent, supreme being who not only creates but directs His creation.

What We Can Know About God

The proofs for God's existence have already led us to a limited knowledge of Him. St. Thomas' Third Way concludes that a necessary being exists which we call God. We have said that a necessary being, unlike contingent beings, has no beginning or end, and that He *must* exist, i.e., he cannot not exist. Another way to say this is that it is of the very essence of God to exist. In other words, essence and existence are not distinct from one another in God. *God's essence is His existence.* That is why He must always exist, without either beginning or end. In all contingent beings, such as human beings, essence and existence are distinct from one another. As we saw in Chapter Two, in all contingent beings, essence is potency and existence is act. Contingent beings are composed of potency and act, of essence and existence. God, on the other hand, is not composed of potency and act. God is pure act. Since there is no potency in God, there is nothing to impose limits on the divine act. That act has no limits. The word we use to express this absence of all limits is "infinity."[18]

The word "infinite" is sometimes used in a different sense by mathematicians. They speak, for example, of an infinite series of numbers. Obviously, any series of numbers is finite, even though one can always add still another number to any series. When we speak of God as being infinite, we are not using this term in its mathematical sense. God is absolutely infinite, not merely mathematically infinite.

We have also said above that God is totally uncomposed. There is in God no composition of potency and act, of essence and existence, of substance and accidents, or any other kind of composition. The word we use to express this absence of any composition is "simplicity." God is infinitely simple.[19]

Furthermore, there can be only one necessary being, one God. If there were more than one necessary being, each would have to possess something which the others lacked. Otherwise, there would be nothing to distinguish them from one another. This would mean that each of them would be a limited being, lacking some perfection or other. And therefore none of them would be infinite. They would all have to be finite beings and, as such, contingent beings. The word we use to express this fact that there can be only one God is "unicity" or, if you prefer, "uniqueness." God is a unique, infinitely simple being.[20] This follows from the fact, established by the Third Way of St. Thomas, that God is a necessary being.

Now we must remember that, in seeking to know as much as we can about God, that we have only our sense experiences of the world in which we live to start with. St. Thomas' Second Way demonstrated that God is the uncaused cause of our world, its Creator. We commonly acquire knowledge of a cause by examining the effect which it has produced. Listening to the music of Mozart tells us a lot about the composer, just as viewing Rembrandt's paintings tells us a lot about the artist. All agree that they were both geniuses. Now we know that a cause cannot produce in an effect any perfection which he himself lacks. So let us examine some of the perfections which we experience in our world in order to increase our knowledge of the Creator who produced them.

To begin with, we experience two types of perfections in the world. There are those perfections which are possessed only by contingent or finite beings such as weight or height or animal sensation, or even human reasoning. By their very nature these perfections are limited or finite. Consequently, we cannot say that God is infinitely heavy, or that He feels things as we do with our senses, or even that He reasons from premises to conclusions as we do. As a matter of fact, we must deny that God possesses these finite perfections, and that very denial teaches us a bit more about Him. We must affirm, of course, that God knows everything in a way which is eminently superior to our way of knowing things. God has unlimited or infinite knowledge.

The second type of perfections which we experience in the world are those perfections which can be possessed by both contingent and necessary beings. Some examples of such perfections are being as being, goodness, truth, knowledge, wisdom, justice, mercy, and so forth. Accordingly we can say that God is infinite being, that He is all good, all wise, all just, and that He possesses infinite or unlimited knowledge.

We must be careful here, however, not to permit ourselves to gain a false knowledge of God. We can never apply any perfection to God and to contingent beings such as ourselves in a way that is totally the same in each case. We must use analogy here, just as we did when predicating our transcendental concept of being of any two real beings, for example of the Pope and of a pebble on the beach. Whenever we attribute to God a perfection which we find in the things of this world, we must do it in a way that is partly the same, but also partly different in each case. Again, philosophers call this "predication by analogy."[21]

St. Thomas says that "the (human) person is the most perfect being in all of nature, it is a being subsisting in a rational nature."[22] Chapter Five will treat the human person in detail. Let us content ourselves here to say that, if, indeed, it is the most perfect being in all of created nature, then most certainly we may predicate this perfection of God, if only by analogy. A divine person is eminently more than a human person. The former is infinite, the latter finite. Yet nowhere in nature do we find anything which so resembles the Creator of nature than does the human person. The one, infinitely simple, necessary being who created the universe we can now identify as our personal God.

4

THE MYSTERIOUS MATERIAL UNIVERSE
(COSMOLOGY)

The "Real" vs. the "Imaginary"

The more material a thing is, the less knowable it is. To know material things, the human intellect must, as we have seen, "dematerialize" them. Our universal ideas are the result of the intellect stripping away from our sense images all the matter which identifies them as individual, material things. Recall here how our sense image of a particular German shepherd becomes our universal idea "dog," which can then be reapplied to any dog of any species existing at any time in any place. And we have also seen that without universal ideas, no science of any kind would be possible.

If things are less knowable the more material they are, it is also true that the more material a thing is, the more imaginable it is. For the imagination is one of the internal senses, and the senses can know only particular material things. Now the human imagination is the most mischievous of all the senses, whether external or internal senses. Sometimes it combines a part of one image with parts of other images to produce fictitious images of things which do not exist at all in the real world. For example, elephants with wings, unicorns, gnomes and fairies. This function of the human imagination has produced mountains of literature which we classify as

mythology and fairy tales. Normally, everyone recognizes that this
kind of make-believe world is sharply distinct from the real world.
But often, in the history of human knowledge, the imagination has
produced images which were quite as false as those of winged
elephants, and nobody recognized that they did not depict the real
world accurately. For example, some primitive peoples imagined
the earth to be a flat disc. Even as late as the 15th century, when
Christopher Columbus set sail from the port of Palos in Spain, some
people suggested that if he travelled far enough westward, that his
three ships would sail off the edge of the ocean into space. Still,
even before Christ, some scientists recognized that the earth is a
globe and not a flat disc. But the shape of the earth was not the only
problem.

A Heliocentric vs. a Geocentric Solar System

It was not until the 16th century that anyone suggested that
the sun does not revolve around the earth, but the earth around the
sun. Nicolaus Copernicus (1473-1543), the Polish astronomer, was
the first to propose a heliocentric, rather than a geocentric solar
system. He died only a few months after he published his theory,
and this timely death spared him from suffering any hostile reactions from the Church and from the academe of his day. Galileo
Galilei (1564-1642), the Italian astronomer, invented the tele-
scope and, with its help, confirmed by his own observations the
findings of Copernicus.

In 1616, the Roman Catholic Church declared the heliocentric theory of Copernicus to be "dangerous to the faith." Galileo was
summoned to Rome and forbidden to teach heliocentrism. Being
a devout Catholic he conformed to the Church's wishes until, in
1632, he published his best known work, A Dialogue Concerning the

Two Chief Systems of the World. This work left no doubt about where Galileo stood on the question. The Church condemned the book and sentenced Galileo to house arrest in Siena. But there could be no turning back. Gradually the whole scientific world, and eventually even the Church, was converted from their geocentric view of the solar system to the heliocentric view of it. And today no one opts for a geocentric solar system. On October 31, 1992, Pope John Paul II publicly apologized to Galileo. He pointed out that Galileo's understanding of the relationship between faith and science was theologically sounder than that of his opponents.[23]

If you are wondering why the Church objected to the heliocentric theory, the answer is intriguing. Theologians taught then, as they still do today, that human beings represent the pinnacle of God's creation within the material universe. The Scriptures proclaim that God created man "a little less than the angels" (Hebrews 2:7). It was unthinkable to 16th century theologians that God would put man anywhere but at the very center of the universe. To say that the earth was a mere satellite of the sun was, to them, to insult the dignity of the human race. Besides, the Scriptures state clearly, these same theologians maintained, that the sun revolves around the earth and not vice versa. They cited passages such as Joshua 10:13 which reads: "And the sun stood still till the people had vengeance on their enemies." Obviously, they reasoned, the sun cannot be the motionless center of the solar system. The earth is.

The Galileo affair was a clear victory for the scientists over the theologians. And the Church learned a valuable lesson, if only very slowly. That lesson is that truth, like being, is, as we have seen, one. No finding of the physical sciences, if accurate, contradicts theological truths. And conversely, no theological truth has anything to fear from scientific research or from its findings. *The truth, like being itself, is one.*

"Fine," you say, "but all of this happened 350 years ago. These are no longer problems today." Are they not? Read on.

Isaac Newton

The same year that Galileo died, an Englishman was born by the name of Isaac Newton (1642-1727). By the time he was 24 years of age, he had become the foremost mathematician and physicist of Europe. Even today, some regard him as the greatest scientist who has ever lived. It was he who discovered the law of universal gravitation, and, together with Leibniz, he is credited with having invented calculus. He was the first to discover that white light is composed of all the colors of the spectrum. He summarized his contributions to both terrestrial and celestial mechanics in his masterpiece, published in 1687, *The Mathematical Principles of Natural Philosophy*. In this work he stated his three laws of motion. Like the Greek Atomists two thousand years before him, Newton saw matter as inert and passive. According to him, if a material body is at rest, it will remain at rest unless it is put in motion by some external force; if the body is moving, it will continue to move at the same speed and in the same direction unless external forces change its speed and/or direction. Matter is, of itself, entirely passive.

In Newton's day, the most sophisticated invention was the clock. The clock embodied for him and for his contemporaries order, harmony, and mathematical precision. And it was by comparison to the clock that Newton described the world in which we live. It is made of inert matter which operates like an immense clock which obeys invariable laws in a totally predictable fashion.

An indispensable part of this Newtonian world-view was the notion of absolute space and time. Newton, and everyone after him until Einstein, imagined space and time to be two, distinct, absolute realities, which were prior to and distinct from material bodies which were described as "existing in space and time." It was as if empty space and passing time were there before anything else existed, waiting for the material universe to come into being. And once bodies exist and begin to move in space and time, that motion can be measured both as to speed and as to direction, and those measurements will remain constant (absolute) no matter who does the measuring from whatever vantage point. Conversely, if, by the wave of some magic wand, one could wipe from existence every last material body in the universe, empty space and passing time would still remain.

Albert Einstein

In 1905, Albert Einstein (1879-1955), then a 26-year-old German physicist working in the patent office in Bern, Switzerland, published a paper containing what came to be known as his "special theory of relativity." In effect, it denied Newton's assertions that motion, space and time were absolutes. Forty-five years later, five years before his death, Einstein published a book entitled *Out of My Later Years*. In it he wrote: "The Principle of Relativity in its widest sense is contained in the statement: 'The totality of physical phenomena is of such a character that it gives no basis for the concept of absolute motion; or, shorter but less precise: there is no absolute motion.'" And if no absolute motion, no absolute space and time.

Einstein suggested experiments which could confirm or contradict his special theory of relativity. One of these experiments was conducted by the noted English astronomer, Sir Arthur Eddington and his assistant, E.T. Cottingham. It involved photographing a solar eclipse which would take place on May 29, 1919. The two astronomers sailed from England to the island of Principe off the coast of West Africa from where they photographed the eclipse.

Simultaneously, other scientists were photographing the same eclipse from the hill town of Sobral in Brazil. The photographic plates confirmed Einstein's prediction that a ray of light glancing off the surface of the sun would be bent by 1.745 seconds of arc, twice the amount of gravitational deflection predicted by Newton's theory. Other experiments suggested by Einstein were conducted subsequently both in Europe and in the United States. All of the results confirmed his predictions based upon his special theory of relativity.

Einstein quickly became the toast of the scientific world, in demand at scores of great universities in Europe and in the United States. From 1933 until 1945 he occupied a chair at the Institute for Advanced Studies at Princeton University in New Jersey. In 1940 he became an American citizen. Einstein was a political pacifist, and he strongly opposed the development and use of the atomic bomb which was made possible by his assertion that all mass has energy expressed in the equation $E=mc^2$. He also deplored the transference of his physical theory of relativity into a theory of moral relativism. There are no longer any absolutes, many people concluded, neither in the physical sphere nor in the moral sphere. Though not a practicing Jew, Einstein believed in the existence of God and he held passionately to absolute standards of moral right and wrong. Having lived to witness moral relativism consume society, and nuclear warfare become the by-product of his fatal equation, he commented shortly before his death in 1955 that there were times when he wished he had become a simple watchmaker.

The Hylomorphic Theory

If, as Einstein says, motion, space and time are not absolute but relative, what are they relative to? They are relative to the material things or the bodies which move, which exist spatially and temporally. Aristotle had something similar to say about motion, space and time. These three are among the accidental forms of being which cannot exist absolutely, but only in a substance. Aristotle called motion "action." Together with space and time, these are three of the nine accidents which, together with substance, comprise the ten categories of being.

Moreover, Einstein explains that the measurements of motion and of space and time are also relative, and not absolute as Newton taught. What are these measurements relative to? They are relative to the particular frame of reference within which the measurer finds himself. An example will make this clear. A train is moving along a track at the speed of 60 miles an hour. Inside the train, a man is walking from one end of a car to the other end of it at a speed of 3 miles an hour. Two onlookers measure the speed of the man's walk. One of these two is inside the train with the walker. He calculates the speed to be 3 miles an hour. The second onlooker is outside the train on the track. He calculates the speed of the man's walk from the point on the track where the walk begins to the point on the track where the walk ends. He calculates the speed of the walker to be 63 miles an hour. All our measurements of the material world and of the bodies which exist in it are always relative to the particular frame of reference within which we make the measurements.

Before we begin to try to explain the physical universe from a philosophical point of view, it is most important that we discipline our imaginations so that they provide us with an accurate image or model of that universe. Otherwise we shall be trying to explain something which is fictitious, something which does not really exist. That is why we have begun this chapter by examining the Newtonian and Einsteinian models of the universe.

From the philosophical point of view, Aristotle and St. Thomas explain the physical universe in terms of what is called the hylomorphic theory.[24] The word "hylomorphic" derives from two

Greek words, "hyle" which means matter, and "morphe" which means form. The hylomorphic theory may be stated as follows: Every real, material being is composed of two elements: first (prime) matter which is pure potency, and substantial form which is a limited act. In receiving the substantial form, the first (prime) matter limits it, just as every potency which receives an act limits that act. The resulting material composite is called by Aristotle and St. Thomas "second matter."

This hylomorphic theory is proposed as an explanation of two physical phenomena which we observe in nature: (1) multiplicity within a species, and (2) substantial change.

We observe in nature countless species of material beings, each of which is possessed by many individuals within that species. It is much easier to identify and give names to living material species than it is to identify and give names to inanimate material species. The human species is the most obvious example. Within the animal and vegetable realms there are innumerable species many of which we encounter every day: German shepherd dogs, Angora cats, termites, carrots, daffodils, the Asian flu virus just to name a few. In the realm of inanimate material beings, things are not so clear. We may speak of the 109 chemical elements which have been discovered to date, and which are recorded on the periodic table. But is it accurate to classify these elements as species? Are iron, zinc, and magnesium, for example, truly species of inanimate, material beings? And what about a rock which I find at the foot of a mountain? The lines which separate one species from another are not nearly so easy to recognize in the inanimate realm of material beings as they are in the animate realm. That probably means that it will be more difficult to offer the hylomorphic theory as an explanation for inanimate, material reality than for animate, material reality. Perhaps the difficulty here lies in the fact that the positive sciences have not yet supplied us with a clear enough model of the inanimate, material world. It is not the responsibility of the philosopher to identify and name species of material beings. Nor is he competent to do so. That responsibility and that competence lies with the positive scientist. A botanist, for example, searches out and identifies plant species. The philosopher merely tries to discover the conditions or causes of their possibility.

As philosophers, we observe that every species contains a multitude of individuals within it. At the present time, for example, there are approximately 5 billion human beings living on this planet. As we have seen in Chapter Two, each one of those 5 billion humans has an individual essence which distinguishes him or her from all the others. Yet those 5 billion essences are strikingly alike one to another. All of them are material, living, sentient, intellectual, free beings. We can only conclude that every human essence is made up of at least two parts: one of these parts is the cause of the individuality or the particularity of the human being. This part we call prime matter. The second part of the human essence is the cause of each human being's likeness to every other human being. This part we call substantial form. The substantial forms of living beings are called "souls." And we experience three kinds of souls in nature: vegetative souls, sentient souls, and human souls. It is the substantial form of a human being, the human soul, which makes that individual being a member of the human species. It is in every case the substantial form of any material composite which places that composed being within a particular species.

We have been speaking of human beings here merely as an example of a species containing many individual members which impels us to propose the hylomorphic theory as an explanation for this natural phenomenon. We could have chosen any species and reasoned in the same way with the same result.

The second phenomenon which we observe in nature which also impels us to propose the hylomorphic theory as an explanation for it is the phenomenon of substantial change. A substantial change takes place in nature each time a substance is transformed into a totally different substance.

The clearest example of a substantial change in nature is the death of any living organism. It is only by observing what a thing does that we know what that thing is. For example: for centuries, farmers have been digging peat from the bogs of Ireland to burn as fuel in the wintertime. Peat is decayed vegetative matter, mainly trees which grew and died in Ireland's primeval forests. The lifeless peat is a totally different substance from the trees from which it was formed. The vegetative soul which activated the tree as its substantial form is lacking in the peat. A new and totally different substantial form activates the peat, an inanimate substantial form. At the same time, there must be something remaining in the peat which was also present in the tree. If this were not the case, we would not have a substantial change, but rather the annihilation of the tree and the creation out of nothing (*ex nihilo*) of the peat. That "something" which is present in both the tree and the peat is the prime matter, the potency which has become a different substance by receiving a different substantial form.

The example of a substantial change which St. Thomas uses is wood which is changed into ashes by fire. Obviously the wood and the ashes are not the same substance. The prime matter remains the same in both substances while each substance is activated by a totally different substantial form.

These two principles of physical being, prime matter and substantial form, are not beings themselves. They are "principles" of being. Each is incomplete and cannot exist apart from the other. Furthermore, they are related to one another by their very natures. When they exist together, there is no third ingredient in the composite holding them together. Together, they constitute a substance, an independently existing corporeal being. When they separate from one another, that substance ceases to exist. If the prime matter receives a different substantial form, it becomes a new substance.

The Principle of Individuation

We have already seen that the cause of the differentiation of the many members of the same species is the matter, while it is the form which causes each member to belong to that particular species. Still, more must be said to explain adequately what it is which individuates each corporeal being.

St. Thomas adopts the explanation offered by Aristotle.[25] The principle of individuation in corporeal beings is not first (prime) matter, but rather "matter signed by quantity." Now quantity, like all the other properties of a body, is conferred by the substantial form. Prime matter is pure potency, totally passive, and receives all its properties or perfections from the substantial form. Yet, as we have also said, the substantial form is what places the being within its species. It would seem that the substantial form cannot be at the same time the principle of specification, which it is, and the principle of individuation. Aristotle and St. Thomas therefore conclude that the principle of individuation within a material composite is prime matter signed or sealed with quantity.

Now a serious problem arises here when we direct our attention to the human corporeal being. In the next chapter we shall see that the human soul, which is the substantial form of the human composite, is a "subsistent" form. That is to say, it is capable of, and actually does survive its separation from the human body. How does it remain an individual without matter and quantity? St. Thomas explains that the separated human soul retains its individuation by virtue of its relation to the human body which it once informed and with which it is destined to be reunited. We have said that no third ingredient is needed to bind the human body and the human soul together. They are related to each other by their very natures. They are made for each other, so to speak. Even in separation from the body the human soul remains what it is — the substantial form of a particular human body.

We saw in Chapter Two that one of the nine accidental categories of being first listed by Aristotle is relation. As examples, we cited my relation to my father, to my house, to my church, to my personal computer. All of these are accidental modes of real being which can exist only when they inhere in a substance. The relation of the human soul to the body is obviously not this kind of a relation. Accordingly, St. Thomas calls it an "essential relation" to distinguish it from an "accidental relation." Some scholastic philosophers, in order to emphasize its special character, call it a "transcendental relation."

Now, if it is true that the human soul is by its very nature essentially correlative to a particular material principle, it is equally true that the soul is individuated by virtue of that fact. This does not differ from saying that the human soul is individuated by its very nature, for it is, by its very nature, the form of a particular body. It is not incorrect to say, as both Aristotle and St. Thomas do, that a material composite is individuated by its matter signed by quantity. But quantity is, after all, an accident which, like all accidents, is conferred on the composite by the substantial form. Ultimately, the individuation of any material being is rooted in its substantial form. And St. Thomas Aquinas himself says so.[26]

As we said at the beginning of this chapter, the more material a thing is, the less knowable it is. Another way to say this is "materiality is inversely proportioned to intelligibility." Using our senses, whether external or internal senses, we can know only individual material things. With this knowledge alone, we could never write a book, or construct a science. To do this, our minds must form and combine many universal ideas such as "potency" and "act," "prime matter" and "substantial form," "substance" and "accident," "space" and "time," "essence" and "existence," "accidental relation" and "essential relation," "life" and "death," "annihilation" and "creation," "individuation" and "specification," "materiality" and "intelligibility." These are some of the universal ideas which we have been using in this chapter to help us in the difficult task of coming to know the mysteries of the material universe.

5

THE HUMAN PERSON
(PSYCHOLOGY)

The Human Person

St. Thomas Aquinas says, as we saw at the end of Chapter Three, that the "(human) person is that which is the most perfect in all of nature; it is a being subsisting in a rational nature."[27] So, to begin with, the person is not the same as the nature. In the last chapter, we spoke of the individuation of natures. And we saw earlier that the terms "nature" and "essence" and "substance" and, in Latin, "quidditas" (in English, "whatness") are interchangeable terms, i.e. they all mean the same thing. A "person" is something else. And, according to St. Thomas, it is more perfect than the nature or the essence. It is also a very mysterious reality and consequently, it is difficult to describe. Nonetheless, we shall now try to describe it.

Every being which exists in the real world must be one. It must be a unified substance which exists by itself, distinct from every other real being. This perfection of unity is not a part of the nature or essence of the being. It is brought to and added to that essence by what philosophers call the "supposit." The English word "supposit" comes from two Latin words: "sub" and "ponere" which mean "to place underneath." The English word "supposit" means the "underpinnings" of the being. What is it that the supposit adds to the nature of the being? All of the following:

1. *existence*: the supposit brings the act of existence, the "to be" to the nature, making it a part of the real world.

2. *unity*: to become a part of the real world, any nature must be one, a perfect unity. As we have seen, the real world is made up entirely of individual beings. Universal essences exist only in our minds as ideas.

3. *accidents*: our universal ideas of natures, or essences, or substances, do not include accidents such as color or quantity. Accidents are added to the substance when the supposit gives the substance existence.

4. *wholeness*: it is the supposit which makes the nature of substance a complete being in the real order, complete as to essence and existence, complete as to substance and accidents.

All of the above apply to every real material being, no matter what its nature, whether non-living or living, whether vegetable, animal or human. But when we talk about the supposits of human beings, we must add something. A human supposit alone is called a "person," and it brings a 5th perfection to the human nature: "who-ness." It is this perfection which St. Thomas describes as "that which is most perfect in all of nature." It is this perfection, this "who-ness" which we identify by assigning a name to it. We say, "this person is John Jones, this person is Mary Smith." And it is to these persons that all the operations of their natures are attributed. For example, it is not Mary's eyes which see, it is Mary who sees by using her eyes. It was not Babe Ruth's arms which hit 60 home runs in the 1927 season, it was Babe Ruth who hit them by using his arms. Similarly, my mind does not think, my will does not decide:

I think and make decisions by using my mind and my free will. The human person is that which is most perfect in the whole of nature.

It is ironic that what is most perfect in all of nature is often the cause of what is most abominable in all of nature. The Latin axiom, "*Corruptio optimi, pessima*" means "The corruption of the best is the worst [corruption] of all." What is the worst in all of nature are the countless acts of injustice and immorality caused by human persons who misuse their freedom. In Chapter Six, we shall examine the rules and standards which nature itself provides to human persons to prevent them from misusing their freedom, and to help them to keep their actions just and moral. But before we get to that, there is more to say about the human person.

The Human Person and the Rational Soul

St. Thomas borrows his definition of the human person from the Roman philosopher, Boethius (475-525), who says that it is "the individual substance of a rational nature." All supposits, even non-human and non-living supposits, are "individual" and "substantial." But only the human supposit is "rational," so we may say that rationality defines the human person. Yet, rationality is a power (faculty) of the human soul which is the substantial form of the material human being. We must now investigate the human soul. In doing so we shall be illuminating our understanding of the human person.

The soul of every human being is unique, incomplete, immaterial, simple, and subsistent:[28]

1. *unique*: Some philosophers, like the Scotch Franciscan, John Duns Scotus (1266-1308), taught that a human being has more than one substantial form or soul: a corporeal form which accounts for the human body,

giving it both existence and life with all its vegetative and sentient functions; and a rational form which adds mental and volitional functions to the human composite. St. Thomas objected that to hold this is to destroy the substantial unity of the human composite. St. Thomas maintains that there is but one substantial form in man, the human soul. It is from this unique human soul that the existence, the corporality, the life, and all the functions of the human being flow.[29]

2. *incomplete*: The human soul is not a being in itself, it is a part of a being (a principle of being). Its nature requires that it exist in union with matter. If the soul were a complete being, the body and soul existing together would not be one being, but two. In that case, the union between the body and soul would not be a substantial union, but merely an accidental union. Nevertheless, we shall see in number 5 below that the human soul can and does exist in separation from the body.[30]

3. *immaterial*: As we have said, we know the nature of a thing by examining its operations. Nothing can produce an operation which is disproportionate to its nature. An axe, for example, can cut down a tree, but it cannot make a bed from the wood. Now in addition to the vegetative and sentient functions of the human soul which are material functions, it also has an immaterial (spiritual) function, the formation of universal, mathematical, and transcendental ideas. Remembering that it is really the human person who does the thinking, these ideas are formed by a process of "de-materializing" the sense images. There is not a trace of matter remaining in the transcendental ideas of being, unity, truth, or goodness. Now the nature which produces these immaterial (spiritual) ideas must itself be immaterial (spiritual).[31]

4. *simple*: Simple means not composed of parts. That the human soul is simple follows directly from the fact that it is immaterial or spiritual. Every substantial form is distinct from the matter which it informs. Extension is a property of bodies, not of forms. So we must conclude that the human soul is unextended, simple, not made up of parts.[32]

5. *subsistent*: To say that the human soul is subsistent is to say that it continues to exist when the body which it informs ceases to exist.[33] Any body, whether human or not, ceases to exist when its parts separate from one another. But the human soul is not a body; it has no parts. Therefore, it cannot cease to exist as a body does. Furthermore, while some human activities such as seeing, hearing, and speaking are totally dependent on the physical organs of the body, other activities such as thinking and choosing are not so totally dependent. It is true that all human knowledge originates in sensation. It is also true that, while the human soul is united with the body, the physical brain is associated with all of its activities. Yet two of these human activities are such that they can take place, when the soul is separated from the body, without the help of the brain. These two activities are knowing and choosing. Accordingly, the human soul is said to be capable of subsisting apart from the body.

A problem arises here in that we said in Chapter Four that it is "matter signed with quantity" which individuates every material composite, including man. If this is so, how does the human soul retain its individuation when it is separated from that matter and quantity? We must recall here that St. Thomas also said that the individuation of the composite is rooted in its form. The human soul, like the substantial form of any material composite, is by its very nature intended to exist in a state of union with matter. It does not lose that identity when it is separated from matter. And once separated from the body, it is destined, St. Thomas teaches, to be reunited with it. Consequently, it retains not only its identity, but also its individuation. Some philosophers put it this way: the separated human soul retains its transcendental relation to the body of which it is the substantial form. This causes it to remain an individual.

Now everything that we can say of the human soul can and must be attributed to the human person who possesses it, with one exception. The human person is not incomplete. In fact, it is the human person who brings, along with existence, completeness to the human composite. The human soul is an incomplete part of that whole. With that single exception in mind, we may now say that the human person is a unique, spiritual, simple, subsistent being. St. Thomas says of it: "It is a being subsisting in a rational nature."[34]

A Look Back at the Whole Human Being

We shall close this chapter by examining the human person in its relation to human freedom. But before we get to that, let us summarize here what we have said in this and in the preceding chapters about the whole human being. In Chapter Two we became acquainted with the Latin word "quidditas" which is translated literally as "whatness." Every dictionary of the English language includes the word "quiddity" which it defines as "the essence; that which makes a thing to be what it is." And we have seen that two additional terms for quiddity and essence are nature and substance.

These four terms are synonyms; each of them describes the same reality, namely the "whatness" of a being. For any "whatness" or essence to exist in the real world, it must receive an act of existence which is brought to it by its supposit. It is the supposit which communicates to the essence existence, unity, and incommunicability. Incommunicability is the perfection which keeps this existing essence distinct from every other existing essence.

Now let us apply this to the human being. We have said that a human essence, like all other essences of material beings, is composed of two incomplete principles of being, prime matter and substantial form. The substantial form of the human composite is the human soul. The human soul possesses powers or faculties on the vegetative level, on the sentient level, and on the rational level. In Chapter One we saw that it is the highest of these powers, the rational faculties, which define the human soul and which distinguish it from every other kind of living soul. And it is because of these higher, rational powers of the human soul, that we give a special name to the supposit which brings existence, unity, and incomunicability to the human essence. We call it the "human person." If we call the human essence, which includes the human soul, a "quiddity" or a "whatness," then we must call the human person a "who-ness" to distinguish it from that essence. Earlier in this chapter we said that the human person, unlike the human soul, is not incomplete. We do not mean to imply by this that the human person is capable of subsisting apart from the human soul. Yet, as we have also seen, the human person can and does subsist in union with the human soul apart from the human body. Still, the whole human being comprises an entire human essence, i.e., prime matter informed by the human soul, possessed and controlled by a human person. And if the human person united to the human soul is capable of subsisting apart from the human body, that must be merely a temporary state of existence, since the human soul is incomplete in itself, and it is intended by its very essence to co-exist in union with matter.

Finally, we have said that all operations of the human essence or human nature must be attributed to the human person to whom we assign a name. It is not Mary Smith's eyes and ears and imagination and mind and will which see and hear and imagines and thinks and chooses; it is Mary herself who does all these things.

The Human Person and Human Freedom

In Chapter One we examined the workings of the human intellect which is a rational power or faculty of the human soul. Now the intellect has a sister faculty, the human will. The object of the intellect, i.e., what the intellect knows, is truth or "being as being." The object of the will, i.e., that to which the will is directed, is goodness or "being as desirable." St. Thomas defines the will as "the intellectual appetite."[35] The will cannot choose anything until the intellect presents the possible choices to it. It is the intellect which first sees the end or goal toward which it then moves the will. And it is also the intellect which provides the will with evaluations of the various means by which the will can achieve that end or goal. Armed with this knowledge, the will then moves freely in a particular direction. Our description here of these two rational activities, knowing and willing, is somewhat imprecise, since we must remember that it is the human person who knows and decides by using these powers of the soul. Strictly speaking, it is not the mind which knows nor the will which decides.

As we shall see in Chapter Six, the final or ultimate end of man is happiness. By its very nature, the human will is directed toward that end. Human freedom consists in choosing the appropriate means to attain that end — happiness. The human will is not free to reject that ultimate end. In this sense we can say correctly that human beings are not absolutely free. In the opinion of St. Thomas Aquinas, who was a theologian as much as a philosopher, human happiness in this life is found in contemplating God; and perfect human happiness, which can be achieved only in the next life, will be found in a direct vision of God. This contemplation and vision of God is man's absolute good. All other ends toward which the will can move are only relatively good insofar as they are related to that absolute good.[36]

The human will is, as we have just said, ordered by a kind of inner necessity to move in the direction of its ultimate end, happiness. However, at the same time, the intellect suggests to the will all sorts of intermediate ends as well as a variety of means by which to attain these intermediate ends. And this is where error and doubt often enter the picture. Both Aristotle and St. Thomas say that "the good is what everyone desires."[37] Yet, what the intellect recognizes and recommends to the will as good is sometimes only apparently good. Sometimes it is actually an evil which the intellect mistakenly sees as a good. It is the human person, of course, who makes these errors of judgment, and it is he or she who is responsible for them. In some cases the mistaken knowledge and the erroneous decisions which follow upon it are not the fault of the person involved. For example, a hunter who shoots his companion, mistaking him for a deer in the forest. In other cases, however, moral guilt is clear. For example, a husband who shoots his wife's paramour, acting out of jealousy and hatred. Yet, even in this latter case, one might claim the presence of extenuating circumstances. Determining moral guilt is often difficult. We shall examine it more closely in the next chapter.

To sum up, the human mind and the human will are sister faculties of the human soul. The will obtains from the intellect the information it needs in order to make right decisions. That is why we speak of "intelligent decisions." That is why St. Thomas calls the will "the intellectual appetite."

A Final Word About "The Human Animal"

Chapter One of this book begins with the words: "The human animal. . ." St. Thomas Aquinas, and many other scholastic philosophers, routinely defined man as "a rational animal." While such definitions are accurate, they can be easily misunderstood. A human being is much more than an animal. He is a personal spirit. He is capable of thinking abstractly and choosing freely, and these operations tell us that he belongs to a world other than the spatio-temporal universe. These rational operations tell us that he survives the death of the body. We find testimony to these facts in the world literature of every period. Here are a few examples:

> "God created man in the image of himself, in the image of God He created him, male and female He created them." Genesis 1:27

> "You have made man a little less than the angels; you have crowned him with glory and splendor." Psalm 8:5

> "I am fearfully, wonderfully made; you knit me together in my mother's womb." Psalm 139:14

> "Man is the measure of all things." Protagoras (485-410 B.C.), ix, 51

> "Thus, while the mute creation downward bend their sight and to their earthly mother tend, man looks aloft, and with erected eyes, beholds his own hereditary skies." Ovid, *Metamorphoses*, bk 1, 1, 84

> 'Twas much that man was made like God before; but that God should be made like man, much more." John Donne, *Sonnet 22*

> "Man is but a reed, the weakest in nature, but he is a thinking reed." Blaise Pascal, *Pensées*, sec. vi, 347

> "Men are not angels, neither are they brutes." Robert Browning, *Bishop Blougram's Apology*

"For smiles from reason flow, to brutes denied."
John Milton, *Paradise Lost*, bk ix, 1, 239

"O man, strange composite of heaven and earth!"
John Henry Newman, *The Dream of Gerontius*, 1, 291

"For a man is not as God, but then most Godlike being,
most a man." Alfred, Lord Tennyson, *Love and Duty*, 1, 30

"Man is a rope connecting animal to superman, a rope over
a precipice." Friedrich Nietzsche, *Thus Spake Zarathustra*,
sec. 4

"Man is the only animal that blushes, or needs to."
Mark Twain, *Pudd'nhead Wilson's New Calendar*

The human person is not only "that which is most perfect in nature," as St. Thomas Aquinas said, he is also that which is unique in all of nature.[38] He is that "strange composite of heaven and earth," as Cardinal Newman called him. Of all the countless beings in the material universe, the human person alone survives death and continues in existence after the material part of him has passed out of existence.

Clearly, the human person has a nobility and a destiny which no other animal shares with him. In the history of the human race, there are many examples of men and women who have carried human knowledge and human choice to great heights of scholarship and holiness. Aristotle and St. Thomas Aquinas are such examples. St. Francis of Assisi in the 13th century, and Mother Teresa of Calcutta in our own inspire universal esteem. And there are thousands of others whom we recognize as having actualized their human potential in very full measure.

There are also, sad to say, striking examples of people who have perverted human knowledge and human choice to an almost unimaginable extent. In the 20th century, Adolf Hitler and Joseph Stalin orchestrated the deaths of tens of millions of human beings. *"Corruptio optimi pessima!"* These were crimes against nature, for nature has its own law which men and women are obliged to recognize and obey. In the following chapter we shall examine the natural law and human behavior.

6

THE NATURAL LAW AND HUMAN BEHAVIOR

(ETHICS)

A Social Animal

Both Aristotle and St. Thomas define man as "a rational animal," but neither of them is content with that definition. Aristotle also says that "man is by his nature a social animal." And St. Thomas repeats this definition.[39] For both of them, human society is the flowering of human nature. St. Thomas expresses this most beautifully in Latin: ". . . *naturaliter, homo homini amicus est,*" "by his nature, man is a friend to man."[40] Four hundred years after St. Thomas wrote those words, another Thomas, the English philosopher, Thomas Hobbes (1588-1679), gave the phrase a fiendish twist: "*homo homini lupus,*" "man is a wolf to man," he wrote. For Hobbes, man was not a social animal, but a brute who would devour all other men to his own advantage, were that possible. Because he finds it impossible, he reluctantly agrees to conform to the laws and customs of an unnatural society, again to insure his own individual interests. But for Aristotle and St. Thomas human society is the natural outgrowth of human nature. Human society is made up of a hierarchy of human communities. The smallest and most basic of these is the family. The family assures the continuation of the human race, and it is necessary for the nurturing and education of the children. Families combine into neighborhoods, neighborhoods into villages and cities, cities into states, and states into nations. None of these communities can function smoothly unless the individuals within it behave ethically. To insure ethical behavior, each community must have an authority structure, laws, and sanctions. In the ideal, utopian community there is no need for sanctions or prisons. But the models of society which Aristotle and St. Thomas described were not fictitious models constructed by their imaginations. The models which they used were models of the real societies in which they themselves lived, models which they knew from their own experience.

The division of labor plays a vital role in the efficient functioning of every human community. There must be rulers, farmers, builders, teachers, and so forth, to promote both the physical and the spiritual growth and well-being of all the people.[41]

Human language is a *sine qua non* of any human society. By its very nature it links the speaker to the listener, the writer to the reader. Language should express the truth, the difference between good and evil, justice and injustice. It is an abuse of language to use it to express falsehoods. Such unnatural use of language can be disruptive of the community and the social order.[42]

St. Thomas found Aristotle's ethics to be correct but incomplete. For Aristotle, ethics was closely related to politics; he described them as "branches of the same discipline."[43] The purpose of the State is to create a framework within which its citizens can live "the good life," i.e., achieve "happiness." Happiness is, according to Aristotle, the highest human good toward which all human activity is aimed. It should not be confused, as it often is, with bodily pleasures. Human happiness consists essentially in the contemplation of truth and the possession of the virtue of wisdom.[44] One achieves happiness by living virtuously —which presupposes sufficient material possessions to insure good health and adequate leisure time. The state must guarantee these to all its citizens. Otherwise, virtuous living will be impossible, and happiness unobtainable.

Although Aristotle sees happiness as man's final end and highest good, he recognizes that men act for intermediate ends and lesser goods. These intermediate goods should never be disconnected from man's ultimate good, happiness. As an example, he cites bridle-making as subordinate to horsemanship, and horsemanship, in turn, subordinate to military science, and military science, in its turn, subordinate to victory. In this context, victory is, for Aristotle, a step toward happiness.[45]

For Aristotle, a moral life is a life of moderation in all things except virtue. Moral virtue can be acquired only through knowledge, self-discipline, and the cultivation of good habits. No human appetite is evil so long as it is indulged intelligently with moderation and discipline.

Although Aristotle's notions of God and of an afterlife are much less defined than those of St. Thomas, he taught nevertheless that man has personal responsibility for his actions.[46] Accordingly, Aristotle devoted the whole of Chapter Five of his *Nicomachean Ethics* to a discussion of the various kinds of justice which must be guaranteed by the appropriate authority within every human community. In the same work, the author exhaustively discusses the intellectual virtues, especially wisdom and prudence, as well as the moral virtues, emphasizing continence and temperance. The subject of Chapters Eight and Nine is human friendship, to which Aristotle attaches great importance in the pursuit of happiness, and which he treats with great delicacy.

From Aristotle to St. Thomas Aquinas

Sixteen centuries separate Aristotle from St. Thomas Aquinas. Aristotle was born in 384 B.C.; Thomas in 1225 A.D. Both were philosophers, but Thomas was also a Christian theologian. Thomas enjoyed sources of knowledge unavailable to Aristotle. Thomas drew much from the Bible, both Old and New Testaments, and he wrote commentaries on many of the Bible's books. He also leaned heavily upon the writings of the early Church Fathers, especially those of St. Augustine. Still, Thomas never confused the two disciplines: philosophy and theology. He recognized philosophy to be a natural science constructed by the use of unaided natural reason alone. Theology, on the other hand, he saw as a supernatural science, the premises of which are divinely revealed. Throughout all of his writings, both philosophical and theological, Thomas cites no one as often as he cites Aristotle. And each of these citations are attributed not to Aristotle by name, but rather to "The Philosopher." For Thomas, Aristotle stood in a class by himself, and compared to Aristotle, no one else deserved, in Thomas' opinion, to be called "The Philosopher."

St. Thomas accepted Aristotle's position that human ethical behavior is based upon the nature of the human being as a "social animal." But for Thomas, this was insufficient. Man is much more than a social animal. He is a being fashioned in the image of the Creator. And that image is the image of a Person who is at once intelligent and free. Like God the Creator, man is a person, he is intelligent, and he is free. Yet the human person is a limited (finite) being, endowed by the totally unlimited (infinite) Creator with limited powers of intelligence and free will.

We must understand clearly here what is meant by creation. Creation, to begin with, is not generation. Plants and animals generate new individuals within their species. Generation is the production of new individuals from some kind of pre-existing material being, from ova and sperm, for example. Creation, on the other hand, is the production of new being from absolutely nothing. It cannot be described as a movement or a motion. For all movement and motion is a passage from potency to act, from something to something else. Generation is a movement from potency to act, from something to something else. Creation is not. Creation is bringing something into being where absolutely nothing pre-existed it. Creation, accordingly, is the act of the infinite, uncaused, first cause, whom everyone calls God. In other words, only God can create.

The Book of Genesis in the Old Testament gives an account of how God created the universe in six days. According to this account He created Adam and Eve, the first human beings, on the sixth day, and He gave them dominion over the whole world. "So God created man in His own image, in the image of God He created him; male and female He created them" (Genesis 1:27).

Creationism vs. Evolution

In our day a debate is raging which Aristotle and St. Thomas did not encounter. The parties to the debate are scientific evolutionists on the one side, and fundamentalist Protestant Christians on the other. The Christians maintain that the theory of evolution contradicts the biblical account of the creation of the human race, and it is, therefore, not a tenable theory. The evolutionists point to the mountain of scientific data which has been amassed in support of the theory of evolution. It seems to be the sort of a debate which admits of no resolution. Since this book makes no pretense at being a work either of Scriptural analysis or of positive science, we do not wish to identify with either side of the debate. Perhaps we can, however, suggest a philosophical consideration which may be helpful.

Evolution is defined as a theory which holds that existing forms of animal and plant life developed by a process of gradual, continuous change from previously existing forms. Living organisms seem to adapt to their environments. This is especially true when an organism passes from one environment to another, for example, from the sea to land. Some evolutionists theorize that all forms of life originated in the sea as a simple, primordial, protoplasmic mass.

The philosophical consideration which we offer here is simply this: If, indeed, evolution has taken place, only material bodies have evolved. Spirits have not and cannot evolve. Furthermore, if it can be shown scientifically that human bodies have evolved from lower forms of animal life related to chimpanzees and orangutans, this will not change the fact that the human soul is a simple, spiritual being, not made of material parts, and consequently not a possible subject of evolution. If the human body has evolved from lower, simpler forms of animal life, it must have reached a point in its development where it was capable of being informed by a human soul. At that point, presumably, God created and infused the soul of Adam into that body. This is merely a theory, but it is not a theory which is inconsistent with Christian theology. The fundamental point here is that only material bodies are subjects of evolution; spiritual souls cannot evolve.[47]

The Vertical and Horizontal Dimensions of Thomistic Ethics

To define the human person as a social animal is to link him horizontally to every other human person with whom he lives in community. In its fullest sense, this definition links every human person to every other human person in the human family.

To define the human person as a being, created in the image of God, the Creator, is to link him vertically to that infinite, creative Being. This vertical dimension is present only faintly, if at all, in Aristotle's ethics. It adds a richness to Thomas' ethics which he expresses in terms of the eternal and the natural law.

St. Thomas accepts the teleological character of Aristotle's ethics, i.e., that man always acts freely for an end which he perceives to be good. And further, that man's final or ultimate good which brings him happiness lies in the contemplation of truth. But Thomas is more specific. The ultimate truth is God Himself. And man's ultimate end which brings him total happiness lies in the contemplation, in the vision of God. Man, who is created in the image of God, finds fulfillment in knowing and loving God in this life, and in being united with Him in the next.

Because God has created the material universe out of nothing, it does not contain within itself the power to sustain itself in existence. God must sustain in existence everything which He brings into existence out of nothing. God is therefore the Lawmaker who preserves and governs what He creates. That eternal law is discoverable, at least in part, by the human person using his natural reason alone. And that discoverable part of God's eternal law St. Thomas calls "the natural law." St. Thomas puts it this way: "It is evident that the natural law is nothing else than the rational creature's participation in the eternal law." And also: "The light of natural reason by which we discern what is good and evil is a function of the natural law which is an imprint on us of divine light."[48]

St. Thomas makes a distinction between the speculative human intellect, the object of which is being as truth, and the practical human intellect, the object of which is being as good.[49] We recall from Chapter One that the speculative intellect knows intuitively, i.e. without any reasoning process, certain basic facts (first principles of being) concerning its object. One of these is "being is not non-being." Similarly. St. Thomas teaches that the practical intellect knows intuitively the basic precept of the natural law which is "do good and avoid evil." It is in the light of that first principle of the natural law which he knows intuitively, that the human person must make all moral decisions. In making those moral decisions, i.e., in applying the first principle of the natural law to specific cases, the human person sometimes errs. In some instances, he is responsible for those errors in moral judgment, in others, he is not. We shall now examine the criteria for making moral judgments.

To begin with, not all the acts of a human person are either moral or immoral. Many are morally indifferent, like walking from one place to another or blowing one's nose. There are some human acts, however, which are said to be "intrinsically evil," i.e., acts which, by their very nature, are seen immediately to be immoral. All agree that incest and murder are examples of such immoral acts. The immorality of these acts is determined by examining the acts in themselves and in their relation to the agent who performs them. The murderer clearly does violence by his act not only to his victim but also to his own human nature. Ethicists sometimes use the term "deontology" to refer to this first method of testing the morality or immorality of a human act.

A second method of testing the morality or immorality of a human act is called "consequentialism." Those opting for this second method contend that one must look to the consequences of a human act to determine whether it is moral or immoral. Some hold that no human act can be said to be immoral so long as it does not harm anyone else.

St. Thomas Aquinas is a deontologist, though that term was not used in his day. He believed that the human person is capable of reading the natural law which the Creator has imprinted on His creatures. In terms of that natural law, human acts may be judged to be moral or immoral. Within the framework of Thomistic ethics, such human acts as homosexuality and abortion are judged to be violations of the human natures of the agents who perform them, quite independently of the consequences which these acts produce. They are classified as intrinsically evil acts.

Still, St. Thomas does not discount completely the consequences of a human act in judging the morality or immorality of that act. He holds, however, that the agent must foresee and intend the evil consequences of his act to be held responsible for them. If a person gives money to a beggar which the beggar then uses for immoral purposes, the act of the almsgiver remains a moral and virtuous act. If a person gives money to a professional assassin to murder an enemy, his act is clearly immoral.

For St. Thomas, the moral content of every human act resides in the intention of the agent. If that intention includes harmful consequences to victims of his act, those consequences contribute to the extent of his guilt. The fact that the agent intends no harmful consequences to anyone as a result of his act does not of itself assure that his act is moral. St. Thomas holds that telling a deliberate lie is an immoral act, whether or not the liar intends any evil consequences to follow from his lie. To St. Thomas, lying is an intrinsically evil act.

The Natural Law and Unnatural Behavior

If St. Thomas is correct in saying that "the light of natural reason by which we discern what is good and evil is a function of the natural law which is an imprint on us of divine light,"[50] then the natural law is a criterion by which we can determine human behavior to be natural or unnatural, moral or immoral. If we believe, for example, that the human person is created in the image of the Creator, that like the Creator he is intelligent and free, then slavery must be seen as unnatural and immoral behavior. For one man to enslave another violates not only the nature of the slave, but also the nature of the master. For master and slave each possess the same intelligent, free human nature. Similarly, dishonesty in politics is a violation of the natural law. When an elected official accepts bribes or kickbacks, he is stealing from the taxpayer who elected him.

Abortion, too, can be seen as a violation of the natural law. Abortion is the deliberate termination of the life of a human foetus. Even if one holds that human life begins somewhat later than at the moment of conception, as St. Thomas Aquinas himself held,[51] one must at the same time recognize that the human foetus is, from the first moment of its existence, ordered by nature to become an intelligent, free, human person fashioned in the image of God. To deprive that human person of his or her right to exist is an unnatural act, a violation of the natural law.

In today's permissive society, many people object to the terms "unnatural" and "abnormal" to describe any kind of human behavior. The simplest way to eliminate these terms from the vocabulary of ethics is to deny the existence of the natural law. If homosexual behavior is considered to be normal when practiced among consenting adults, or if it is considered to be normal simply because it is practiced by 2 percent of the population, then no further criteria remain by which we can determine whether this type of behavior is in harmony with or in violation of human nature. This kind of thinking denies the vertical dimension of ethics which is the basis for the existence of the natural law.

The Rule of Reason — The Virtues

Following his mentor, Plato, Aristotle gives great importance to the cultivation of virtue in pursuit of "the good life," in pursuit of happiness. All human powers, e.g., the mind, the will, the imagination, the emotions are controlled and perfected by the cultivation of the virtues. Virtues are learned and acquired by the human person by repetitive good acts. Vices, on the other hand, are learned and acquired by repetitive evil acts. Since reason is the highest human power, it should rule all the other human powers, assuring that they function in a way which leads the human person to his proper end which is happiness. The highest virtue of the human intellect is the virtue of wisdom. This virtue empowers the human person to lock his focus on his ultimate end. The wise human person makes all the choices of his life by relating them to the ultimate good of his life — happiness. Aristotle speaks also of moral virtues which relate more to the human will than to the intellect. These are justice, courage, and temperance.

St. Thomas accepts this Platonic-Aristotelian view of the natural virtues while adding extensively to it. As a Christian, he recognizes a second kind of virtue of which the Greeks had no suspicion, namely, supernatural virtue. Supernatural virtues are the free gift of God to His human creatures. They are not acquired by repetitive acts; they are infused into the human person by the Creator. These are primarily the virtues of faith, hope, and charity, which Christians believe God infuses into everyone who receives the sacrament of baptism. Although these three virtues are not acquired by repetitive acts, they are activated and intensified by repetitive acts of faith, hope, and charity. The function of these supernatural virtues is to unite the human person, by supernatural grace, to God the Father through His divine Son, Jesus Christ, the Redeemer.[52]

But at the same time, St. Thomas, following Aristotle, teaches that there are natural virtues which control and perfect the natural powers of the rational creature.[53] Several such virtues relate to the intellect. These are principally wisdom, prudence, understanding, science and art. Wisdom is the supreme virtue because it focuses on the highest causes, especially on God who is man's last end. Prudence, in St. Thomas' words, is "right reason about things to be done."[54] Prudence steers a middle course of right reason between the two extremes of excess on the one hand and of deficiency on the other. For example, the virtue of prudence might prompt a person to undergo a physical examination once a year to preserve good health.

Other natural virtues relate primarily to the human will rather than to the intellect, and these are called the moral virtues.[55] Aristotle lists the principal moral virtues as three: justice, courage, and temperance. St. Thomas adopts these, but he prefers to call courage fortitude. He treats each of them at length, enumerating numerous subdivisions of each of the three. Chastity, modesty, and humility are, for example, moral virtues each of which is a kind of temperance. All the moral virtues are exercised under the aegis of the intellectual virtues of wisdom and prudence.

AFTERTHOUGHTS

Realism vs. Idealism

The most basic question in all of philosophy is this: "Does a real world exist apart from my knowledge of it?" Another way to ask this question is: "To what do my universal ideas correspond?" The answers which philosophers have given to this question have led to two positions which are diametrically opposed to one another: realism and idealism. Following Aristotle and St. Thomas, many philosophers have answered that my universal ideas correspond to the material objects in the real world from which my mind abstracted them in the first place. For example, my universal idea "dog" corresponds to the natures (essences) of each of my three dogs, Prince, Pal, and Petunia, from which my mind abstracted the idea. It also corresponds, of course, to all other dogs which have existed in the past, which exist in the present, or which may exist in the future. That is why I call it a "universal" idea and why it is such a useful tool in expanding my knowledge of the real world in which I live.

Beginning with René Descartes (1596-1650), philosophers began to abandon Aristotelian-Thomistic realism. Although he thought of himself as a realist, Descartes held that certain of our universal ideas come to us not from our sense contact with the material universe, but rather from God. These are "innate" ideas which are "clear" and "distinct" and are, consequently, "true." The truth of my innate ideas is guaranteed by the source of them, God Himself. Descartes mistrusted sense knowledge, and frequently said so. In his *Sixth Meditation* he wrote: "And, indeed, as I perceive different sorts of colors, sounds, odors, tastes, heat, hardness, and so forth, I safely conclude that there are in the bodies from which the diverse perceptions of sense proceed, certain varieties corresponding to them, *although, perhaps, not in reality like them.*" And in his *Principles of Philosophy*: ". . . by our senses, we know nothing of external objects beyond their figure, magnitude, and motion."

The English philosopher, John Locke (1632-1704), carried Descartes' position further by distinguishing between primary and secondary qualities of material bodies. A body's primary qualities (one of which is mass) are the essential qualities which make up the nature (essence) of that body. Secondary qualities, on the other hand, such as color, sound, odor, and so forth, belong not to the body which is known, but rather to the human being who knows the body. Alfred North Whitehead (1861-1947), the English mathematician and philosopher, a convinced realist himself, has commented on this Lockean view of the universe: "Nature is a dull affair, soundless, scentless, colorless, merely the hurrying of material, endlessly, meaninglessly."[56]

A bit later, a Scotsman, David Hume (1711-1776), struck another blow at realism by insisting that we cannot perceive, and therefore we cannot know, the relation of an effect to its cause. Our only perception is of succession in space and time. One thing exists before another thing does. But there is no justification for concluding that the former is the cause of the latter. Hume would say that the gas flame over which I place a pan of water cannot be known to be the cause of the heating of the water. The flame was there before I placed the pan of water over it. That is the only conclusion I can draw.

But it was a German, Immanuel Kant (1724-1804), who sounded the death knell of realism. Fascinated by Hume's ideas ("I freely confess that it was the thought of David Hume which, many years ago, first interrupted my dogmatic slumbers and gave an entirely new direction to my inquiries in the field of speculative philosophy"),[57] Kant commented that "the concept of connection between cause and effect is by no means the only one through which the understanding thinks connections between things *a priori*." By this he meant that the world as we know it (which he called the "phenomenal" world) is structured not only by the secondary sense qualities of Locke, not only by the causal intelligible category of Hume, but by every category into which we classify the world in knowing it: color, odor, taste, time, space, substance, accidents, relationships, action, passion, and so on. The "noumenal" world (which is the world as it exists in itself, apart from our knowledge of it), does not fall into any of these classifications. It is a totally unstructured world to which human knowledge has no access whatsoever. I do not *discover* the world, as the realists maintain, I *invent it*. Whitehead said of this 18th century idealism: "It has held its own as the guiding principle of scientific studies ever since. It is still reigning. Every university in the world organizes itself in accordance with it. No alternative system of organizing the pursuit of scientific truth has been suggested. It is not only reigning, but it is without a rival. And yet it is quite unbelievable."[58]

There is a lot at stake here. As we mentioned at the end of Chapter Three and again at the beginning of Chapter Five, St. Thomas Aquinas says that "the (human) person is the most perfect being in all of nature."[59] Man is the pinnacle of God's creation, "made," as the Book of Genesis tells us, "in the image and likeness of God." But a man, living in the ideal world of Descartes, Locke, Hume, and Kant is a very different creature than a man living in the real world of Aristotle and St. Thomas. To begin with, in the real world the human mind discovers the causal links between effects and their causes. This enables it to reason to the existence of God as the first cause of all the finite effects which are perceptible in the world. In an ideal world, the human mind invents or fashions the finite objects which it cannot conclude are effects of any cause. In an ideal world, there can be no rational proofs for the existence of God.

It is equally difficult in an ideal world to find any rational basis for human freedom. St. Thomas explains that God is not only the Creator who brings the universe into being out of nothing, but He is also the Conserver of everything He creates. A finite being does not contain within itself the power to preserve itself in being. That requires an infinite power just as does creating out of nothing. As the Conserver of creation, God is also the Lawmaker who governs what He creates. That eternal law of God is discoverable by man, at least in part, by his use of his natural reason alone. And that discoverable part of God's eternal law St. Thomas calls "the natural law." On this point St. Thomas writes: "The light of natural reason alone by which we discern what is good and evil is a function of the natural law which is an imprint on us of divine light."[60] If, as Kant maintains, we have no intellectual access to the "noumenal world," i.e. the world-in-itself as God has created it, then it becomes impossible to discover in that world a natural law.

A vigorous effort has been made in the 20th century to revive Aristotelian-Thomistic realism which had lain dormant for more than 500 years. In 1889, at the request of Pope Leo XIII, Monsignor (later Cardinal) Mercier of Belgium founded the Institute of Philosophy at the University of Louvain to focus its attention on the study of medieval philosophy, especially on the thought of St. Thomas Aquinas. For more than a century, this Institute at the University of Louvain has been publishing a profusion of philosophical literature with emphasis on the history of philosophy. The names of two Frenchmen are intimately connected to the neo-Thomistic movement of the 20th century which was initiated at

Louvain. They are Jacques Maritain (1882-1973) and Etienne Gilson (1894-1978). Maritain, after converting to Catholicism while still a student at the Sorbonne in Paris, devoted his whole life to a study of Thomism and of its application to all aspects of contemporary life. He strenuously opposed idealism which he accused of abandoning the proper function of the human reason. Among his numerous writings special attention should be given to his *Preface to Metaphysics* and his *Approaches to God*. Gilson championed the notion of a Christian philosophy, asking his contemporaries: "What makes pagan philosophy more of a philosophy than Christian philosophy?" He is the author of *The Christian Philosophy of St. Thomas Aquinas* and of *The Spirit of Medieval Philosophy*. Both Maritain and Gilson lectured widely in North America. Gilson founded the Institute for Medieval Studies at the University of Toronto (1929). A similar Institute honoring Maritain has been established at the University of Notre Dame.

Yet another voice has been heard recently calling for a return to realism. It is the voice of Pope John Paul II. In his book *Crossing the Threshold of Hope*, which first appeared in the United States on October 20, 1994, he attributes the de-Christianization of Europe to "modern immanentism and subjectivism":

> "We find ourselves on the threshold of modern *immanentism and subjectivism*. Descartes marks the beginning of the development of the exact and natural sciences as well as of the humanistic sciences in their own new expression. He turns his back on metaphysics and concentrates on the philosophy of knowledge. Kant is the most notable representative of this movement.

> "Though the Father of modern rationalism (Descartes) certainly cannot be blamed for the move away from Christianity, it is difficult not to acknowledge that he created the climate in which, in the modern era, such an estrangement became possible. It did not happen right away, but gradually.

"In fact, about 150 years after Descartes, all that was *fundamentally Christian* in the tradition of European thought *had already been pushed aside.* This was the time of the enlightenment in France when *pure rationalism held sway.* The French Revolution, during the reign of terror, knocked down the altars dedicated to Christ, tossed crucifixes into the streets, introduced the cult of the goddess reason. On the basis of this, there was a proclamation of *Liberty, Equality, and Fraternity.* The spiritual patrimony and, in particular, the moral patrimony of Christianity were thus torn from their evangelical foundation. In order to return Christianity to its full vitality, it is essential that these return to that foundation." [61]

Writing on Descartes' rationalism on an earlier page of his book, Pope John Paul comments:

"How different from the approach of St. Thomas (Aquinas) for whom it is not thought *which determines existence, but existence, "esse," which determines thought!* I think the way I think because I am that which *I* am — a creature — and because He is He who is, *the absolute uncreated Mystery.* If He were not Mystery, there would be no need for Revelation, or more precisely, there would be no need for God to reveal Himself." [62]

The idealism of Immanuel Kant closed all the windows of access which the human mind had had to the real world. The Institute of Philosophy at the University of Louvain together with Jacques Maritain, Etienne Gilson, Pope John Paul II and many others have been trying to reopen those windows. That this book will contribute in some small way to that effort is the hope of its author.

ABOUT ARISTOTLE
AND ST. THOMAS AQUINAS

Although their births were separated by 16 centuries, Aristotle and Thomas had much in common. They were both born into affluent families. They were both endowed with prodigious intelligence. They were both superbly educated men. They were both teachers and writers. They shared the same *weltanschauung*, i.e. the same apprehension of the world and of how the human mind knows the world. Who was the greater of the two? Without hesitation, Thomas would answer: *"Aristotle!"*

Aristotle

Aristotle was born in 384 B.C. at the town of Stagira in Macedonia which is today the northernmost province of Greece. His father was the court physician to the King of Macedonia, Amyntas III. Amyntas was the grandfather of Alexander the Great whom Aristotle tutored beginning in 342 B.C. when the Prince was 13 years old and his tutor 42. Aristotle, realizing that he was training the future King, instructed his pupil in the superiority of the Greek culture and civilization. Non-Greeks were thought of by the Greeks, including Aristotle, as barbarians. This was particularly true of the Persians whom Alexander conquered in 333 B.C. From Persia the Macedonian army moved on into India where Alexander died at the age of 33 in 323 B.C. Although he was, in the cause of pan-Hellenism, the greatest conquering general of ancient times, Alexander the Great did not revere his tutor. Aristotle was deeply disappointed when Alexander married a Persian noblewoman and pressured his fellow officers to do the same. Even more hurtful to Aristotle was Alexander's ordering the execution for treason of Aristotle's nephew, Callisthenes of Olynthus, in 328 B.C. on an expedition into Persia. Callisthenes had been Alexander's chronicler on that expedition.

Because his father was a doctor, Aristotle's initial intellectual interest was in the medical sciences and biology. He gradually expanded these interests into many other fields including astronomy, physics, logic, rhetoric, art, politics, ethics, metaphysics, psychology, and poetry.

At the age of 17, Aristotle enrolled in Plato's Academy at Athens which was permeated by the memory of Socrates who had been executed unjustly by the Athenian State only 15 years before the birth of Aristotle. Aristotle remained associated with the Academy for twenty years. Had he been selected to succeed Plato as the head of the Academy, Aristotle probably would have stayed on in Athens. But when Plato's nephew, Speusippus, was given the post, Aristotle, at the age of 37, began a 12 year period of travel.

He went first to Assus, a newly established town on the Asian side of the Aegean Sea in what is now Turkey. He founded a "philosophical circle" of friends and associates there and led them in a study of political philosophy and ethics. After 3 years, he transferred to the Greek island of Lesbos which is located close to the Turkish coast, and he set up another "philosophical circle" at the island's capital, Mytilene. There he shifted the focus of his attention to plant and animal biology. In 343 B.C., King Philip II invited Aristotle to Pella, the capital of Macedonia, where he spent the next three years tutoring Philip's son, Alexander the Great. In 339 B.C. he returned to his mother's estate at his hometown of Stagira. He remained there in quiet study until 335 B.C. when, at the age of 50, he returned to Athens and set up a school, the Lyceum, to rival Plato's Academy. The Lyceum flourished under Aristotle's direction for the next 12 years and continued on for more than 250 years after his death.

When Alexander the Great died in 323 B.C. some of the Athenians provoked anti-Macedonian agitation, and it became dangerous for Aristotle, himself a Macedonian, to remain in Athens. It was said at the time that he withdrew from Athens to prevent the Athenians from "sinning twice against philosophy." This was a reference to the execution of Socrates which had taken place 77 years earlier. He fled to Chalcis on the Greek island of Euboea where he died the following year (322 B.C.) at the age of 63.

Aristotle was widowed once and married twice, siring a daughter, Pythias, whom he named for his first wife, and a son, Nicomachus, by his second wife whom he named for his father. His *Nicomachean Ethics* is named for his father and his son. His second wife survived him, and he provided generously for her in his will. "In recognition of the steady affection she has shown me," he wrote. Twice happily married, Aristotle commented: "As for adultery, let it be held disgraceful for any man or woman to be found in any way unfaithful once they are married and call one another husband and wife."

Two hundred fifty years after Aristotle's death, Cicero in his *Academica* wrote of "the suave style of Aristotle, a river of gold." Time has washed away that river of gold. The 47 surviving works of Aristotle are written in a clipped style, and consist of Aristotle's lecture notes transcribed and edited by his students. Ancient catalogs list 170 works attributed to Aristotle; many of these are lost, while others are component parts of his surviving works. Four of Aristotle's works are particularly relevant to the content of this book. They are:

1) *The Categories*

2) *Metaphysics*

3) *On the Soul*

4) *The Nicomachean Ethics*

It is difficult to exaggerate Aristotle's importance in the emergence of Western thought. He gave it a realistic orientation which has endured to the present, surviving the challenges of British empiricism and Kantian idealism in the 17th and 18th centuries. No other philosopher since Aristotle has contributed more than he to the development of what is termed "Western Civilization." That is why St. Thomas Aquinas always referred to him as simply "The Philosopher."

Thomas Aquinas

Aquino is a small town in central Italy located midway between Rome and Naples, close to the ancient Benedictine Monastery of Monte Cassino. There, in 1225 Thomas was born to Landolfo, the Count of Aquino and his second wife, Theodora of Chieti. Thomas was the youngest of seven brothers, the eldest three of whom had been born to Landolfo's first wife. Thomas also had five sisters. At that time the border line separating the Papal States from the Kingdom of Sicily ran just north of Aquino. Landolfo was an official in the service of Frederick II, the King of Sicily and the Holy Roman Emperor. Frederick feuded with a succession of six Popes, asserting his imperial authority over the Papal States, until Pope Innocent IV excommunicated him from the Church in 1245.

Landolfo and his family were faithful Roman Catholics and they frequently found themselves on the razor's edge between allegiance to their King and fidelity to their Pope. Several of Landolfo's sons served in Frederick's armies, and one of them, Rinaldo, was executed by Frederick for sedition. Rinaldo was venerated as the family martyr.

At the age of five, Thomas was placed in the Monastery school at Monte Cassino. At the age of fourteen, his education was interrupted when, in 1239, Frederick banished the monks from Monte Cassino and occupied it with his soldiers as a fortress. After spending a few months at the family castle, Roccasecca, where he had been born, Thomas was sent off to Naples to continue his education. There he met Dominican priests and brothers who were dedicated to the intellectual life and to preaching.

It is worth noting here that the Dominicans had been founded in 1216 by Father Dominic de Guzman to preach against the Albigensian heretics who held that matter is evil and that Jesus possessed only the appearance of a physical body. About the same time (1223), Francis of Assisi founded the Franciscans to work among the poor. The founding of these two religious groups marked the beginning of the Mendicant Orders in the Catholic Church. Mendicant Orders combine the monastic life with active apostolates, and their members vow themselves to evangelical poverty, possessing neither private nor community property.

Thomas was strongly attracted to the Dominicans and offered himself to them as a candidate for the priesthood in 1244, when he was 19 years of age. When the news reached the ears of Thomas' mother, she was outraged that her youngest son had joined a group of "beggars." She traveled immediately to Naples where she was told that Thomas had been sent to Rome. When Theodora of Chieti reached Rome, she discovered that Thomas had left Rome on foot with a group of Dominicans heading for Bologna. She dispatched instructions to her older son, Rinaldo, later martyred, who was billeted at the town of Terni along the route to Bologna. Rinaldo intercepted Thomas and delivered him to their mother back at Roccasecca. Theodora imprisoned Thomas in the family castle and pressured him with threats and promises in an attempt to shake his resolve to become a Dominican. She did not succeed and, after a year's captivity, she permitted him to travel to Paris where he rejoined the Dominicans. It was the autumn of 1245.

At Paris, Thomas came under the tutelage of the Dominican scholar, Albert the Great. When Albert was transferred to Cologne in 1248, he took his young student along with him. Thomas continued his studies under Albert's supervision until 1252 when he returned alone to the University of Paris to complete the work for a Master's degree in Theology. He obtained it in 1256 and remained as a Professor at the University for the next three years. Quickly, he acquired a reputation as an influential intellectual, and, in 1259, Pope Alexander IV invited him to become a consultant and lecturer to the Roman Curia. He worked in this capacity for ten years, first at Anagni, then at Orvieto, and finally at Rome, serving three Popes. It was during this period at Rome, in the Dominican convent of Santa Sabina, that Thomas wrote the major part of his principal work, the *Summa Theologica*.

Thomas' voluminous writings fall into five categories:

1) His two major works, the *Summa Theologica* and the *Summa contra Gentiles*.

2) His commentaries on books of the Bible, both the Old and the New Testaments and on the *Sentences* of Peter Lombard (the standard manual of theology used at European universities at that time).

3) His *Disputed Questions* which are accounts of his teaching at the University of Paris and in Italy.

4) His *Opusculae* (little works) which are brief reactions of Thomas to questions which arose during his teaching career.

5) His Latin poetry including Eucharistic hymns as well as the Mass for the feast of Corpus Christi which he was commissioned to compose by Pope Urban IV.

In the Fall of 1269, Thomas was sent back to Paris where he became embroiled immediately in a divisive doctrinal debate which had just exploded on the University scene.

Averroes (1126-1198) was an Arabian philosopher from Moorish Spain whose commentaries on Aristotle were just at that time coming to the attention of the Parisian theologians. Averroes, himself a Muslim, taught that there were two truths, a truth of reason and a truth of faith, and that sometimes they may contradict one another. This was acceptable neither to the Muslims nor to the Christians. Yet Averroes won many disciples at Paris. And Thomas engaged them in debate. He accused Averroes and his disciples at Paris of misinterpreting Aristotle. He argued that philosophy and theology are distinct sciences which, when properly pursued, never contradict one another. Human reason has its own laws according to which it knows the truth without any supernatural interventions. Naturally known truth may be supplemented by divine revelation, but the former is never contradicted by the latter.

This was a new doctrine to the ears of many Catholic authorities, and they felt threatened by it. There was a Catholic tradition which traced its origin back through St. Augustine (354-430) to the Neo-Platonists, which held that the human mind must be divinely illumined in order to know the truth. Thomas did not sympathize with such a line of thought.

The Bishop of Paris finally condemned radical Averroism in 1277, three years after Thomas' death. Yet this condemnation did not exonerate Thomas. Some of the propositions held by the Averroists and condemned by the Bishop were accepted by Thomas. So the condemnation touched parts of his teaching, at least by implication. Happily, in 1272, Thomas' Dominican superiors extricated him from this unpleasant atmosphere at Paris, asking him to set up a Dominican center of studies at the University of Naples. It was to be Thomas' last assignment. He set up the center where he continued to lecture and to write until December 6, 1273, the feast of St. Nicholas. A fellow Dominican who assisted Thomas at Mass that morning, Bartholomew of Capua by name, reported what happened: "After the Mass, he never wrote nor dictated anything, in fact he hung up his writing instruments." When asked by his secretary and associate, Brother Reginald, why he had given up writing and lecturing, Thomas responded: "I cannot go on. . . All that I have written seems to me like so much straw compared to what I have seen and what has been revealed to me." It would seem that Thomas had some sort of mystical experience, perhaps accompanied by a physical breakdown. His health deteriorated quickly from that day onward.

Unaware of Thomas' failing health, Pope Gregory X summoned him to the Second Council of Lyons in Southern France. Thomas, accompanied by Brother Reginald, began the long journey from Naples to Lyons in early March of 1274. They traveled only a few miles to the town of Maenza when Thomas fell gravely ill. Sensing that the end was near, he asked Brother Reginald to take him to the nearby Cistercian Abbey at Fossanuova. It was there that he died on the 7th of March, 1274. He was not yet 50 years of age. Only 49 years after his death, in 1323, Pope John XXII canonized Thomas at a triumphal ceremony which was held at Avignon, France during the period of the so-called Babylonian Captivity (that is, the period when the Pope was based in Avignon rather than Rome). Two years later, the Bishop of Paris, Stephen Bourret, revoked the condemnation of 1277, issued by his predecessor, Stephen Tempier, "insofar as it touched or seemed to touch the teaching of Blessed Thomas." From that day to this, many Popes have endorsed the teaching of St. Thomas Aquinas. In 1567, Pius V, himself a Dominican, appointed St. Thomas a "Doctor of the Church," describing him as "the most brilliant light in the Church." In 1879, Leo XIII declared the philosophy of St. Thomas Aquinas to be the official philosophy of the Catholic Church and required that all candidates for the priesthood be schooled in it. This endorsement was reinforced when, in 1918, Thomas' name was inserted in the Church's Code of Canon Law. Canon 1366, paragraph 2 legislates that candidates for the priesthood be trained "according to the method, doctrine, and principles of the Angelic Doctor."

The Angelic Doctor, Thomas, was greatly indebted to Aristotle for "the method, doctrine, and principles" which he taught. It is thought that Thomas first read Aristotle's works as a teenager while studying in Naples. The natural wisdom of Aristotle's world vision and his analysis of human knowledge had a profound formative effect on the keen young mind of Thomas. Aristotle's world view became Thomas' world view. In a sense, Thomas was a more comprehensive scholar than Aristotle. For Thomas was a Christian theologian as well as a philosopher. Christian revelation suggested many topics to Thomas which were unknown to Aristotle, as for example the Trinity of Persons in the Godhead. But the orientation of Aristotle's thought, which is often described as "moderate realism," permeated every recess of Thomas' mind, and it is as present in his theological writings as in his philosophical writings. Without Aristotle, Thomas would have been a very different kind of scholar. Without the two of them, our contemporary world would have been very different.

ABOUT THE NOTES

When, on December 6, 1273, St. Thomas Aquinas "hung up his writing instruments," he left unfinished his masterpiece, the *Summa Theologica*. Although he wrote it for his students, "beginners," it was this work which attested to his genius, and which gave theology the status of a legitimate science for the first time in history. It is from this work that most of the notes in this book are drawn.

The *Summa Theologica* is a lengthy, comprehensive study of the nature of God, the nature of His created universe, both material and spiritual, and particularly the nature of man which bridges the material and the spiritual created universe. In composing it, St. Thomas followed the format for major treatises which was employed at that time at all the major European universities. The *Summa Theologica* (S.T.) is divided into three *Parts* (I, II, III).

The second of these three parts is so long that it is subdivided into "the first *Part* of the second *Part*" (I-II) and "the second *Part* of the second *Part*" (II-II). Each *Part* is divided into *Questions*; for example, *Question* 2 of *Part* I is entitled: "The Existence of God." Each *Question* is divided into several *Articles*; for example, *Article* 3 of *Question* 2 in *Part* I is entitled: "Whether God Exists." To refer to this particular *Article* footnote 9 will read: S.T. I, 2, 3., i.e., the first *Part*, the second *Question*, the third *Article*. Each *Article* begins with *Objections*; for example, "It seems that God does not exist because . . ." Following the *Objections*, St. Thomas quotes an authority which supports his position. These authorities include the Sacred Scriptures, the Fathers of the Church (e.g., St. Augustine), Aristotle, etc. Then St. Thomas states his own position which always begins with the words "I answer that. . ." After stating his position, he answers succinctly each of the *Objections*.

If the above appears to be unnecessarily complicated, it is nonetheless necessary and can be simplified by an example. Footnote 42 referring to St. Thomas' definition of man as a "social animal" is: S.T. II-II, 109, 3, ad 1. This footnote is read: *Summa Theologica*, the second *Part* of the second *Part*, *Question* 109, *Article* 3, answer to the first *Objection*.

Five other works of St. Thomas are cited in the footnotes:

1) *Summa contra Gentiles* (S.c.G.) This is St. Thomas' second most important work. Written much earlier than the *Summa Theologica*, it was intended not for students, but rather to explain Christian beliefs to unbelievers. It is divided into four *Books*, each of which is divided into *Chapters*; for example, footnote 26 reads: S.c.G. II, 83, i.e. *Summa contra Gentiles, Book* 2, *Chapter* 83.

2) *De Veritate* (De Ver.) This treatise "On Truth" was one of the "Disputed Questions" on which St. Thomas lectured weekly at the University of Paris. It is divided into *Questions* and *Articles*; for example, footnote 11 reads: De Ver. I, 1 , i.e. *De Veritate, Question* I, *Article* 1.

3) *De Ente et Essentia* This marvelously lucid short treatise "On Being and Essence" which Thomas wrote while still in his twenties for his fellow Dominican students is divided into *Chapters*; for example, footnote 24 reads: *De Ente et Essentia, Ch.* 2.

4) *Commentary on the Metaphysics of Aristotle* (In Meta.) St. Thomas wrote commentaries on the twelve *Books* of Aristotle's *Metaphysics* as well as on several other of "The

Philosopher's" works. Our footnotes contain only one
reference to these Commentaries, viz., footnote 10: In
Meta. Bk. 5, #1 through #30.

5) *De Principiis Naturae* (On the Principles of Nature) St.
Thomas addressed this brief work ("Opusculum" in Latin)
to his "Brother, Sylvester," probably a fellow Dominican
student whom Thomas was tutoring. In it Thomas treats
the intrinsic and extrinsic causes of natural bodies. The
citation we have taken from it (footnote 7) hints at St.
Thomas' talent for poetry.

NOTES

1. S.T. I, 84, 6: As he does frequently, St. Thomas refers in this Article to the works of Aristotle, viz. *Metaphysics*, Bk. 1, # 1.

2. S.c.G. II, 83.

3. S.T. I, 3, 4.

4. In Meta. Bk. 5, #14.

5. *De Ente et Essentia.*

6. S.T. I, 13, articles 5 and 6.

7. *De Principiis Naturae*, Ch. IV, #24.

8. Ibid.

9. S.T. I, 2, 3.

10. Aristotle's *Metaphysics*, Bk. V., #1 - #30; St. Thomas, In Meta. Bk. V.

11. De Ver. I, 1.

12. S.T. I, 5, 4, ad 1; De Ver. 21, 1.

13. S.T. I, 48 and 49.

14. S.T. I, 48, 1.

15. S.T. I, 2, 1, ad 2.

16. S.T. I, 3.

17. Aristotle's *Physics*, Bk. 8; In Meta. Bk. XII.

18. S.T. I, 7.

19. S.T. I, 3, especially article 7.

20. S.T. I, 11, especially article 3.

21. S.T. I, 44, 1; S.c.G. I, 32; De Ver. XXIII, 7, ad 9.

22. S.T. I, 29, 3.

23. See *Religious Faith Meets Modern Science*, by Paulinus F. Forsthoefel, S.J. (NY: Alba House, 1994), p. 19. Galileo's major theological statement is his *Letter to the Grand Duchess Christina*, which may be found on pp. 173-216 of *Discoveries and Opinions of Galileo* (tr. and ed. by Stillman Drake) (NY: Doubleday, 1957).

24. *De Ente et Essentia*, Ch. 2.

25. *De Ente et Essentia*, Ch. 2; S.c.G. II, 83.

26. S.c.G. II, 83; S.T. I, 76, 2, ad 1.

27. S.T. I, 29, 3.

28. S.T. I, 75, 2.

29. S.T. I, 76, 1.

30. S.T. I, 76, 3.

31. S.T. I, 76, 8.

32. S.T. I, 75, 1.

33. S.T. I, 75, 2.

34. S.T. I, 29, 1.

35. S.T. I, 19, 1.

36. S.T. I-II, 1, articles 5 and 7.

37. S.T. I-II, 10, 2.

38. S.T. I, 29, 3.

39. Aristotle's *Nicomachean Ethics*, Bk. I, Ch. 7, 1097b; S.c.G. III, 17.

40. S.c.G. IV, 54.

41. S.c.G. III, 134.

42. S.T. II-II, 109, 3, ad. 1.

43. Aristotle's *Nicomachean Ethics*, Bk. X, Ch. 9.

44. Ibid., Bk. X, Ch. 8.

45. Ibid., Bk. I, Ch. 1.

46. Ibid., Bk. III, Ch. 1.

47. For more on this, see *Religious Faith Meets Modern Science*, referenced in note 23.

48. S.T. I-II, 91, articles 1 and 2.

49. S.T. I, 79, 11, ad 2.

50. S.T. I-II, 91, articles 1 and 2.

51. S.T. I, 76, 3, ad 3 and I, 118, 2, ad 2.

52. S.T. I-II, 62.

53. S.T. I-II, 57.

54. S.T. I-II, 57, 4.

55. S.T. I-II, articles 58, 59, and 60.

56. "The Century of Genius" from *Science and the Modern World*, by Alfred North Whitehead (NY: New American Library, 1948).

57. Immanuel Kant, the *Introduction to the Prolegomena to Any Future Metaphysics*.

59. S.T. I, 29, 3.

60. S.T. I-II, 91, 2.

61. *Crossing the Threshold of Hope*, by Pope John Paul II (NY: Alfred A. Knopf, 1994), pp. 51-52.

62. Ibid., p. 38.

BIBLIOGRAPHY

Adler, Mortimer J. *Aristotle for Everybody*, Macmillan Publishing Co., Inc.: New York, NY, 1985.

_____ *Six Great Ideas: Truth, Goodness, Beauty, Liberty, Equality, Justice*, Macmillan Publishing Co., Inc.: New York, NY, 1981.

Barrett, William and Aiken, Henry D., Editors. *Philosophy in the Twentieth Century*, Random House: New York, NY, in 4 vols., 1962. Volume 2 contains an essay by Alfred North Whitehead entitled "The Century of Genius" which is chapter 3 of Whitehead's book *Science and the Modern World.*

Copleston, F.C., S.J. *Aquinas*, Penguin Books: London and New York; first published in 1955, reprinted in 1991.

Davies, Paul and John Gribbin. *The Matter Myth*, Simon and Schuster: New York, NY, 1992.

Forsthoefel, Paulinus F., S.J. *Religious Faith Meets Modern Science*, Alba House: Staten Island, NY, 1994. This book addresses the Evolutionist-Creationist debate.

Gilson, Etienne. *The Spirit of Medieval Philosophy*, translated by A.H.C. Downes, Charles Scribner's Sons: New York, NY, 1936.

_____ *God and Philosophy*, Yale University Press: New Haven, CT, 1941.

_____ *Being and Some Philosophers*, Pontifical Institute of Medieval Studies, Toronto, 1949.

_____ *The Christian Philosophy of St. Thomas Aquinas*, translated by L.K. Shook, CSB, Random House: New York, NY, 1956. Gilson includes in this book the complete catalogue of the works of St. Thomas Aquinas composed by I.T. Eschmann, OP; it lists 98 works, some few of which may be apocryphal.

_____ *Moral Values and the Moral Life: the ethical theory of St. Thomas Aquinas*, translated by Leo Richard Ward, Shoe String Press: Hamden, CT, 1961.

_____ *The Spirit of Thomism*, P.J. Kenedy: New York, NY, 1964.

_____ *The Unity of Philosophical Experience*, Charles Scribner's Sons: New York, NY, 1965.

_____ *Thomistic Realism and the Critique of Knowledge*, translated by Mark A. Wauck, Ignatius Press: San Francisco, CA, 1986.

Hawking, Stephen W. *A Brief History of Time: from the Big Bang to Black Holes*, Bantam Press: New York, NY, 1988.

John-Terry, Chris. *For the Love of Wisdom: An Explanation of the Meaning and Purpose of Philosophy*, Alba House: Staten Island, NY, 1994.

Maritain, Jacques. *The Rights of Man and the Natural Law*, translated by Doris C. Anson, Charles Scribner's Sons: New York, NY, 1943.

_____ *A Preface to Metaphysics*, Sheed and Ward: New York, NY, 1948.

_____ *Approaches to God*, translated by Peter O'Reilly, Harper: New York, NY, 1954.

_____ *St. Thomas Aquinas*, translated by Joseph W. Evans and Peter O'Reilly, Meridian Books: New York, NY, 1958.

_____ *The Degrees of Knowledge*, translated from the 4th

French edition by Bernard Wall. Charles Scribner's Sons: New York, NY, 1959.

McMullin, Ernan, ed. *Evolution and Creation*, Notre Dame University Press: Notre Dame, IN, 1985.

Phelan, Gerald. *St. Thomas and Analogy*, The Aquinas Lecture. (1941), Marquette University Press: Milwaukee, WI.

Polkinghorne, John. *One World: The Intersection of Science and Theology*, Princeton University Press: Princeton, NJ, 1987. A nuclear physicist of high regard in England, John Polkinghorne turned his attention to theology and was ordained to the Anglican priesthood. Few others are as qualified to discuss the relation of science to religious faith.

Rahner, Karl. *Science and Christian Faith*, in *Theological Investigations*, vol. 21, translated by Hugh M. Riley, Crossroad Publishers: New York, NY, 1988.

INDEX